The Dream Betrayed

The Dream Betrayed

Religious Challenge of the Working Class

Karen L. Bloomquist

Fortress Press   Minneapolis

THE DREAM BETRAYED
Religious Challenge of the Working Class

Scripture quotations unless otherwise noted are from the Revised Standard Version of the Bible, copyright © 1946, 1952, and 1971 by the Division of Christian Education of the National Council of Churches.

Cover design: Eric Walljasper
Cover illustration: Caroline Goytia

Library of Congress Cataloging-in-Publication Data

Bloomquist, Karen L., 1948–
    The dream betrayed : religious challenge of the working class /
Karen L. Bloomquist.
        p.   cm.
    Includes bibliographies and index.
    ISBN 0-8006-2323-1
    1. Church work with the working class—United States.   2. Church
and labor—United States.   3. Social classes—United States.
    4. Sociology, Christian—United States.   I. Title.
    BV2695.W6B66   1989
    261.8'34562—dc20   89-12071
                                                                          CIP

The paper used in this publication meets the minimum requirements of American National Standard for Information Sciences—Permanence of Paper for Printed Library Materials, ANSI Z329.48-1984.   ∞ ™

Manufactured in the U.S.A.   AF 1-2323

94   93   92   91   90   1   2   3   4   5   6   7   8   9   10

to the unsung working-class saints of
St. Stephen, Faith, and St. Philip
Lutheran Churches, who helped me to
see, hear, feel, and ask why . . .

and especially to Bill and Aaron,
who sustained me as I tried to make
sense of it all.

Contents

Preface

In recent years central theological understandings have been questioned, challenged, and transformed in light of the different experiences and struggles of African Americans, Latin Americans, women, and a variety of other peoples around the world. Various liberation theologies have resulted.

This book can be associated with these developments. It is primarily a reenvisioning of theology and a reconstruction of sin and redemption in the light of an analysis of class realities in American society.

Its focus is on the experience of American working-class people, particularly those who are white, who have often been perceived as opponents of these other struggles for liberation. They constitute two-thirds of those employed in the United States, and the majority of many congregations. Yet their experience in society and in the church usually has received very little attention in theological thought.

Class generally has not been taken seriously as a category of analysis in this society. We have assumed we are a classless society, thereby ignoring the painful reality of class for many persons. In this book *class* is understood not as a static position in the social order, but as a pervasive dynamic that affects all of us. Thus the particular interpretation of working-class experience that is set forth here may resonate with the experience of many who do not think of themselves as working class. Furthermore, some who are working class may take issue with aspects of the interpretation developed here, which is intended to evoke ongoing attempts to revise our understandings of the particularities of working-class experience.

This book began to emerge a decade ago while I was doing doctoral work at Union Theological Seminary, New York City, and at the same time pastoring a working-class congregation. It is an attempt to put those two realities in dialogue with one another. My primary debt is to the many working-class persons in my upbringing and pastoral experience, whose reality I often scorned and whose pain I often overlooked. I am appreciative to those at Union who gave me the space and encouragement to pursue this project, especially Tom Driver, Dorothee Soelle, and Beverly Harrison. But most of all, I am appreciative of the "long-suffering" endured by my husband Bill and son Aaron as this book came to birth.

Karen L. Bloomquist

1

Introduction

The weight of class

> can be lifted only by transformations of the self
> comparable to those described in earlier eras by
> words like *redemption* or *salvation.*

—*Richard Sennett and Jonathan Cobb* [1]

Many people who cling to the promise of the American
dream—that you can be upwardly mobile if you try hard
enough—have experienced a profound sense of betrayal in
recent years. Although the dream continues to be fulfilled
for some, for many others the signs that cause uneasiness and
disillusionment are all too apparent:

- Between 1978 and 1986, the middle income group in the
  United States shrank from 52.3 percent to 44.3 percent of
  the population. One-third of those who left moved to
  higher income levels, but two-thirds fell into lower levels,
  in contradiction to the promise of the American dream. [2]
- Communities, families, and individuals who have worked
  hard to get ahead economically have been devastated

11

by the closing of factories that provided their economic sustenance.

- Many farmers have lost or remain in danger of losing their family farms.
- During the 1980s, approximately 20 million more non-agricultural jobs were created in the labor market. Nearly all of this growth was in the service sector, while manufacturing and other goods-producing jobs declined in number.[3]
- More persons in the United States are now employed by low-paying McDonald's fast-food franchises than by the entire steel industry. Over half the jobs created since 1980 fail to lift families from poverty. Eight million more people are poor.[4]
- The "good life" that many parents have desired for their children, particularly owning their own home, is out of reach for an increasing number of young working-class families.

The sad irony is that those who are devastated and despairing continue to succumb to rhetoric that perpetuates the illusion of the American dream but fails to address these underlying realities. Many people hang on, hoping that the worst has passed.

And in the midst of this, where is the church?

Most predominantly white churches continue to articulate the Christian faith in ways that remain untouched by the implications of these developments in the lives of working people. Churches provide sympathy and reassurance to those who are affected, but are at a loss to know how to change the situation.

Many churches have responded to some of the resulting social-service needs. Congregations have opened food pantries, begun support groups for the unemployed, tried to avert individual home or farm foreclosures, and even organized job retraining programs. A few have become advocates of public-policy initiatives, such as legislation that discourages plant closings. A growing number of people in the church and society are recognizing that work is undergoing a radical restructuring. Concerns for persons and for the future shape of communities are likely to be overlooked, unless public outrage is expressed and more just alternatives considered. Such efforts are crucial. The specific focus of this book, however, is on the spiritual and theological challenge inherent in this situation. How can our pastoral and theological understandings and practice be reconceived so that those who have been and continue to be victimized might be empowered and work together to transform their situations? Economic and political changes will be more effective if they relate to the actual experiences, cultural values, and ideologies that uphold the present order and provide the framework of meaning for working people. By beginning to understand such dynamics, we discover some deeply spiritual and theological issues are at stake, issues that communities of faith are uniquely equipped to address.

Such a task is important for several reasons. White working people have been among the staunchest believers in the way American society and its institutions are structured. An appeal for social justice that challenges such structures is not likely to be well received. Social-justice appeals have often been presented in such a way that they appear antagonistic to these workers' interests. The wounds of class, which have not been taken as seriously as those of race or sex in the United States, are embedded in white working-class antagonism toward the struggle for justice by women and people of color.

The dynamics of class, often pitted against the dynamics of race and sex, must be understood and analyzed on their own terms so that we can move beyond and replace the divisive appeals that presently haunt us with more effective, interconnected political strategies. For this reason, this book's primary focus is on the reality of white workers, although much of the analysis is applicable to other racial or language groups that are caught up in the same dynamics, sometimes in an even more desperate attempt to make it in American society. Furthermore, much of the data is taken from the experience of those who either are male, or define themselves in relationship to men. How can we better understand this experience in the aftermath of an era in which the greatest increase of inequality has been among nonblack men?[5]

Until today's real crisis of working people's spirit is exposed, and connections are made between their personal pain and wider structural realities, their potential solidarity with those more commonly perceived as oppressed here and around the world will not be realized. Becoming active historical agents in the midst of their situation will not occur until the contradictions between the dream and the reality of their lives are exposed. This painful process is energized when persons are grasped by another reality—a transformative, communal religious vision.

My interest in this area arises out of eight years of parish ministry among working-class parishioners. I regularly struggled with the challenge of proclaiming grace in the face of the realities of sin in which their lives were immersed. From them I heard the perennial human longing: to be treated as persons rather than objects. I became conscious of the ever-more-desperate ways in which working persons struggle to assert their humanity over and against those people and historical forces that deny them their dignity and worth.

For the good news of the gospel to become real for such persons, at least three entrenched dualisms need to be challenged. The first is the tendency to separate God, the active subject, from human beings, the passive objects of God's activity. Rather than viewing human activity as in competition with God's activity, human beings need to be viewed as co-subjects with God, mutually active in the world. Second, the tendency to separate a spiritual realm from the social-economic-political realm needs to be challenged. The spiritual dimension of life does not move persons out of the world of historical realities but more deeply into those realities, there to be shapers of greater justice, engendering a fuller humanity for all. Third, ministry that tends to deal with the pain of persons and communities at only an individual level, must go further. To be fully *with* persons in their pain, to be truly incarnational in ministry, leads to questioning and challenging the social-economic-political order that causes and contributes to the pain. The personal dimension is part of a total social situation involved in historical change.

The pastoral dimension of ministry is also necessarily prophetic. As the biblical prophets demonstrated, immersion in the pain of the people leads to a prophetic, political, often confrontational ministry lodged in the heart of a God who suffers with people. Herein lies a redemptive drama with public—social, economic, and political—ramifications.

2

The Dilemma of Working People

Who Are Working People?

The stereotypical urban working-class neighborhood is familiar—rows of modest houses, mostly owner-occupied and well kept, often with aluminum siding and plastic trim in colors set off from their neighbors'. Inside the well-trimmed yards, flowers grow, occasionally interspersed with religious statuary, patriotic flags, or ornamentation imitative of far more expensive houses. On summer evenings, occupants sit on their front steps, chatting with and calling to one another, while neighborhood youngsters play ball in whatever space is available, perhaps even the street. The husbands sit inside, in front of television sets, drinking beer, occasionally yelling out commands or obscenities to their wives, children, or buddies outside. The people's lives revolve around this community, providing them with a sense of who they are and what they value.

"Working folks" is the common self-designation of those who would identify themselves as "working class" in most societies.

Because the American dream makes no class distinctions in its promise, generally class designations and consciousness have been less clear-cut than in Europe. Here, most of the working class strives to be seen as middle class in its values and material culture. This designation tends to include nearly everyone—except the poor or "underclass"—and works against the emergence of class-conscious interests. On this basis, some social scientists maintain that "class" is not an important social dynamic in the United States. Ethnicity and race are viewed as more central.

Those who are uncomfortable identifying themselves as "working *class*," however, do tend to think of themselves as working *people*, indicating a reality they have in common. This reality is, in fact, class-based. It is shaped by their experience in the workplace but permeates nearly all of their life, resulting in distinct life styles, self-images, and cultural values. Class is a crucial factor in defining how people see the world, their place in it, and their response to it. Whether a person is employed in a working-class job is not crucial if one identifies with the working-class values, ethos, and ideologies. Thus, retired persons and offspring are likely to be shaped by this reality for a generation or two after the head of the household has held a working-class job. Furthermore, farmers, often romanticized as working for themselves, are increasingly finding themselves victimized by socioeconomic factors beyond their control, in ways similar to working-class persons in cities and towns.

Within the working class, emphasis falls on the positive virtue of working rather than on class specification. Work is the route to dignity by making something of oneself. Yet work is *labor*, not something to be enjoyed. One grins and bears it because it is better than "not working." A clear sense of demarcation exists between working people and those who don't work. Those who don't work are the hard-core unemployed or those whose jobs involve less menial labor, more independence, creativity, and social status—whose jobs are not "work" in the sense of the mindless drudgery that is common among working people. As one laborer observed, "When you've a job where there's some call for planning, some call for figuring things out . . . you feel you're in a different class from the fellow who handles things."[1] Working people are acutely aware of the difference between themselves and pastors or other professionals, regardless of those persons' backgrounds, suspecting that such individuals lack a sense of the real world as working people experience it.

A primary distinction is between working class and managerial or professional jobs, or between manual labor and mental labor. In an era when clerical and retail sales workers have increasingly become the production workers of our economy, traditional distinctions such as collar color are no longer decisive.[2] Studies have substantiated the increasing similarity between factory work and both office and retail sales work, in which manual speed and dexterity dominate the labor process as a whole.[3] Much white-collar clerical work is becoming increasingly a domain of manual labor or production, in which a small set of computer-related functions are performed repetitiously.

Working class today includes blue-collar workers (both skilled and less skilled) and those in the growing service sector of the labor market (pink-, gray-, and some white-collar jobs). Typically in these jobs, little developed skill or training is required (except for some skilled blue-collar workers), nor is there much control over what one produces or much opportunity for advancement. Those in the service sector prepare and serve food, clean, protect and care for others; they include both retail sales clerks and clerical workers in offices. Their incomes typically are low. In 1988 the median weekly earnings of clerical workers was $308; sales workers, $222; and service workers, $232. Due in part to the historic influence of unions, blue-collar skilled workers earned $430, and those less skilled, $313.[4] In 1986 these workers together

19

constituted approximately 62 percent of employed males and 70 percent of employed females, a clear majority of the work force in the United States.[5]

These persons and their families are the main reference for the designation, *working class*. More people than these, however, tend to think of themselves as working people, and share in the distinct values and life orientation (for example, agricultural workers). Because of the current reshaping of the labor market, and especially the significant growth in service sector jobs, more and more jobs are acquiring working-class characteristics. Hence, we can speculate that greater numbers of persons will continue or begin to think of themselves as working people.

The Hope and the Reality

The central theme or hope in working people's lives is, *I* can make it if *I* try hard enough. The belief in individual achievement through perseverance is the overriding rule in American society. This individualism is motivated by the promise embedded in the American dream that this is the land of unlimited opportunity where anyone's son or daughter may become the equal of "the boss's son or daughter."

In this "effortocracy," which is the current version of the American dream, downward mobility is viewed as punishment for the "sin" of not trying hard enough. As the hoped-for triumph is in our own hands, so, too, is the dreaded humiliation. Those who *have* deserve what they have, and those who *have not* just need to try harder. It is a dream that "divides us in reality even as it unites us in fantasy"; "it encourages us to 'dream up' in good times and 'blame down' in bad."[6] Disparities in income and status are viewed as transitory and due to the individual's effort or lack thereof, rather than due to structural factors.

In this "individual-as-central" framework,[7] when achievements do not measure up to aspirations, a person compensates by:

- blaming the disparity on an impeding situation over which one has little control, for example, the economy or job market;
- lowering one's personal aspirations so that they are more in line with one's actual achievements ("I never wanted to be more than a ditchdigger");
- inflating or counterfeiting one's achievements to convince oneself and others that one really has not fallen short, for example, buying consumer goods that are more typical of a higher class, or deflating others' achievements; or
- contrasting one's relative "success" with those who are more visible "failures," in order to feel superior to "them."

Some of "them" are working people who are "hard livers."[8] Hard livers are more cynical about the American dream, realizing that they are not going to make it. They are often rebellious and willing to fight to defend their pride and identity as individuals. They tend to be highly suspicious of social-political-religious institutions and of professionals. They are frequently scorned by their siblings or cousins who are "settled livers."

Settled livers have a greater sense of rootedness, with more stable families and greater pride in home. They tend to be regular, reliable workers, and cautious, conservative churchgoers. Their lives are built around the promise of the American dream. They resent those who have not "made something of themselves" and who are painful reminders of the precariousness of their own settled-living ethos.

In juxtaposition to the American dream is the crass reality of many working people's lives today: the experience of
downward mobility, despite allegiance to "effortocracy."
The dream is of a classless society, the reality is one of classism. The dream is that one can shape one's situation, the
reality is that one feels victimized by forces that leave one
passive. Farmers hear their parents say, "We got through the
'30s, why couldn't you get through the '80s?" Workers are
shocked to find that as individuals they are far less the deter-
miners of their destiny in society than they had assumed.

That painful realization strikes home when factories
close and farms are foreclosed. Millions who staked their lives
on "making it" find themselves without a livelihood or resort
to jobs at one-fourth or less of the unionized wages they previously made. They find themselves on the same level as the
"welfare bums" they used to look down upon. For more and
more working people, the American dream has been betrayed. Persons, families, communities, and regions of the
country are being shattered. John Raines and Donna Day-
Lower diagnose the crisis:

> Only rapid economic growth has made the American dream a be-
> lievable promise, feeding the hearts and minds of the majority with
> a slowly improving life-style, while leaving unaltered the underly-
> ing division of wealth. But then came the new economic realities of
> the 1970s and 1980s. . . . The American dream—that anybody
> can become somebody—does not serve well as a guiding vision in a
> period of slow economic growth and a shrinking middle class. In
> hard times the dream invites self-blame rather than structural eco-
> nomic analysis. And in sustained hard times it encourages a disas-
> trous distortion of conscience that finds satisfaction in taking it out
> on the poor while continuing to dream, forlornly, of someday—"if
> not me, then my kids"—making it to the top.[9]

Working people's reality is one of increasing pathos. To
understand better the contradictions between their dream

and the reality of their lives—how the dream has been betrayed—we need to ask, Why is it like this? and then analyze some of the key historical and structural factors in the present situation.

What Is "Work"?

Most working people do not like to talk about their work. The job is something to do, not to talk about, especially at church. Although there is dignity attached to the fact that one is working, there generally is little inherent meaning or dignity in the work itself, even if it has a respectable title, such as "sanitation technician" (i.e., garbage collector). When I asked my parishioners about their work, they often changed the focus to what they do when they *leave* work, exhausted and relieved. A job is something one puts up with. For example, a retired railroad worker replied that what he liked about his job was "nothing"; it was "work"; when he left work he felt "better"; and he envied people who "have jobs they like."

Pervasive feelings that working people have about their jobs are that they are boring, monotonous, dull, and permit little individual expression. As one worker shared, "God, I hated that assembly line. I used to fall asleep on the job and still keep doing work. There's nothing more boring and repetitious in the world."[10] Consequently, workers develop ways to break the monotony by joking or playing around or finding ways to "beat the system" in order to endure.

Many workers report "feeling like a machine," with the irony that machines are usually worth far more and sometimes cared for better. Not only might the machines end up taking away a worker's job, but if one keeps the job, one ends up doing something even more machinelike. This is the case for factory workers as well as for an increasing number of clerical

23

workers. As more of labor is governed by classified motions that extend across the boundaries of trades and occupations, its concrete forms dissolve into types of work motions, which are easily replaceable. This sense of feeling replaceable is even more striking because of the physical health dangers long associated with many blue-collar jobs. Breathing in dust, developing black-lung disease in the mines, or losing one's limbs in industrial accidents are some of the more obvious dangers. But industrial jobs are no longer the exclusive domain of such dangers. Farming has replaced mining and quarrying as the nation's most hazardous occupation. Questions are being raised about the safety of the computerized office, especially the video display terminals. VDT workers (80 percent of whom are women) appear to have a higher incidence of problems with vision, muscles, stress, and fatigue, as well as some evidence of greater damage to human fetuses.[11]

Many workers would not identify all of these problems with *their* particular job, but one common feeling is the sense of being controlled by those above them. Regardless of a job's objectives, how closely one is controlled by the boss, manager, or work process determines how strongly one feels a part of the working class.

Working people are, by definition, those who are under the control of others. Control is exercised through a variety of means:

- close supervision, such as the data entry operator's machine being monitored by the supervisor;
- specific rules and policies that must be followed;
- direct, public measurement of a worker's output;
- restrictions on physical movement, governed by a time clock or bell;
- fear of losing one's job by stepping out of line.

Workers' pervasive experience of being controlled or dominated is the central phenomenon of their work lives. This results in a sense of powerlessness. The dream is that they are in charge of their destiny. The reality is that others control whether, how, for how much, and with what security they will work. Many workers assume that moving upward means escaping from this dilemma, but those who do often discover that control operates more insidiously, making them feel more powerless. How did this come to be?

The Evolution of Workplace Control in American Capitalism

We need to analyze the evolution of control in the workplace to understand how subtle and pervasive this control has become. During the past century the United States has become dominated by monopoly capitalism rather than a competitive system of small entrepreneurs. The concentration of capital allows giant corporations to decisively shape the economic order, the workplace, and class relations. These corporations exercise an inordinate control over plant locations, jobs, wages, prices, profits, products, and the work process. Such centralization of capital occurs through various types of mergers and takeovers.

The growth of a large managerial stratum has been crucial within giant corporations. Management's role is to control the labor process, a control legitimized through formal knowledge and education. Workers view managers as the authorities who unravel how and why things happen. Some observers see them as mediating the basic class conflict of capitalist society.[12] Yet their position is ambiguous. Managers are expected to represent the corporation's interests, but they ultimately lack total control over the production process.

Hierarchical Control. In nineteenth-century small businesses, *simple* control[13] was exercised by means of the entrepreneur's personal control and authority over his or her workers. Such control was informal and unstructured. As firms grew, *hierarchical* control by supervisors and managers was necessary. Workers performed their tasks correctly or were docked in pay, fired, or sometimes beaten. Early unions organized in reaction to such arbitrary means of control.

Today it is ironic that jobs under simple and hierarchical control are the least likely to be unionized. This is the so-called secondary labor market of casual jobs where labor is treated as a commodity. These are low-paying, low-security, high-turnover, dead-end jobs with few if any prerequisites or benefits: fast-food workers, store clerks, low-level clerical workers, guards, janitors, low-level hospital workers, and migrant agricultural workers.

A disproportionate number of women and minorities are employed in such jobs. A family whose primary wage earner works in this sector is likely to be among the working poor. This accounts, in large part, for the correlation of poverty with race and for what has been called the "feminization of poverty."[14] From 1960 to 1984, the number of poor female family heads increased 83 percent.[15]

The growth of the service sector depends upon the continued availability of a supply of workers not presently in the labor market, or who have been squeezed out of higher paying jobs. As the pool of cheaper labor evaporates, service sector employers may be forced to pay higher wages.

Structural Control. In contrast, the primary labor market usually offers more job security, with more stable employment patterns, higher wages, and better defined occupations with established patterns for advancement. The so-called subordinate primary jobs are the traditional unionized working-class jobs in factories, offices, and stores. Age, experience, and schooling are more important. Although workers are less subject to arbitrary firings, there is little protection against the adverse effect of wider company policies, for example, the decision to close a plant.

Structural control prevails in this labor sector. Originally such control was instituted to deal with workers' discontent. It is not based on power directly exercised by human beings, but power made invisible within the structure of the work. Companies began providing fringe benefits, spelling out formal procedures for filing grievances, and using principles of "scientific management" to structure the work process. Under the latter, control over the labor process passed from the workers to the machines, which imposed the rhythm. This was epitomized in Taylorism, which dictated to workers the precise manner in which work was to be performed and in what amount of time. The labor process became disassociated from the workers' skills. The brain work of conception was separated from the manual work of execution, in a mind/body dualism. Craft knowledge was systematized and concentrated under the control of employers, who doled it out in the form of instructions needed to perform a task. Although technology is not inherently oppressive, in some cases it became the immediate oppressor, with workers having even less control over their work lives. In today's computerized technology work is evaluated as well as monitored by the machine.

Bureaucratic Control. Technical means of control require another element of structural control, namely, the modern corporation's *bureaucratic* control, which becomes embedded in the firm's social and organizational structure. This form of control began in the white-collar office, but has increasingly moved to more blue-collar production work. The impersonal face of company rules and company policy becomes the basis for control, with carefully delineated and stratified job classifications, wage scales, and job responsibilities. Rules carefully spell out the requirements for adequate job performance, with automatic incentives built in for those who do the job well. Power appears to emanate from the formal organization. Rather than the "us versus them" climate prevalent when control is more directly imposed, workers are persuaded to see themselves as part of the company family. They are reconciled to the firm's power, goals, and values. The firm becomes a social institution. To attack it is to attack society itself.

These forms of subtle control operate most often in the independent primary labor market, where there is more independence, initiative, and self-pacing, along with extensive bureaucratic control. Employees include: long-term clerical, sales, and technical staff; craft workers in the trades; and professionals (including those in the church). Experience, age, and education are crucial. It is not surprising that well over 70 percent of the people in these jobs are white males.[16]

Do these workers see themselves as working people? Although they sell their labor like others, their subjective experience of being controlled is far different. Their interests and the firm's interests are felt to be compatible. As long as a company is doing well economically and shows concern for the worker as a person, this interpretation is credible. The worker's soul or identity becomes tied to the company. He or she counts on the firm for future security.

But when these workers lose their jobs, not because they failed to measure up to the bureaucratic rules but because a company moves or shuts down, they also feel betrayed by the company. Then the possibility exists for exposing the real interests that are at stake in this labor market and for aligning these workers and their interests with the more overtly controlled workers. However, such solidarity comes slowly because the class distinctions based on their having "made it" are so entrenched, and the ideological underpinnings of bureaucratic control are so powerful. Furthermore, education, culture, and values have given them a different interpretation of their work experience. They are more apt to see themselves as middle or upper middle class than as working people.

Workers' Responses to Being Controlled

British researchers have identified three responses of the working class to being dominated.[17] First are the "proletarianized workers," who see themselves as part of a community of solidarity with other workers. Unionism and the "boss versus worker" distinction are crucial. By 1995 it is projected that less than 10 percent of the work force in the United States will belong to unions.[18] Many of the workers are cynical about any worker solidarity, and work force growth is primarily in nonunionized sectors. Proletarianized workers constitute a decreasing proportion of working people.

A second, more common phenomenon, especially among churchgoers, is that of "deferential workers," who staunchly believe in hierarchy, individualism, commitment to the company, and in the possibility of upward mobility. They are likely to be obedient to authority, amenable to certain right-wing appeals, and committed to a moral order that legitimizes their subordination. They are "good" workers—loyal to the boss and the patterns of control in the workplace.

In contrast, "privatized workers" tend to be indifferent toward the job, the boss, and other workers. Their main motive for working is material acquisition—what the paycheck makes possible. They have little concern for class cohesion or hierarchical social status. Commodity-consciousness prevails over authority-consciousness. There is low ego involvement in the workplace, with identity and status based instead on acquiring things or leisure-time activities.

Depending on their different worldviews, value systems, resources, and perceptions of the situation, the workers' responses to the control they experience in the workplace will vary dramatically, and in ways more nuanced than the three types cited above. But what they experience in the workplace will likely shape the way they perceive and relate to the world.

Workers typically experience a sense of "surplus powerlessness."[19] The real, objective powerlessness is structured into the world of work, family, and childhood in such a way that people end up overestimating their powerlessness. Surplus powerlessness is the set of feelings and beliefs that make people think of themselves as even more powerless than they are, and leads them to act in ways that actually confirm their powerlessness. This process of accommodating to an oppressive situation, believing that nothing can be done to change it, becomes generalized throughout life and leads to a repression of who human beings are created to be.

The biblical understanding of work is that it should express who and whose we are. Work is meaningful in and of itself. It sustains us, not because of the income it produces, but because the activity of working is basic to who we are as human beings: cocreators with God and with one another. We pour ourselves into our work so that the product of our labor might express who we are. But work as most workers experience it is far from this.

People are powerless to the extent that they are prevented from actualizing their human capacities, particularly in their work situation. Stress is one way persons experience their powerlessness. Anger is directed inward. Studies indicate that when workers feel powerless in their jobs, there is a greater risk of psychic distress and coronary disease.[20] American working people are strongly conditioned to view what happens to them as due to what they as individuals have done or failed to do, so self-blame is common, even when what has occurred is not their fault. Through such self-blame, workers disempower themselves and work against rather than with one another in the struggle to change their work conditions. The work situation is one of alienation, which carries over into how workers are likely to respond to the rest of their world—as given and unchangeable.

Alienation

Understanding the manifestations and ramifications of alienation is crucial for comprehending why working people seem so immobilized in their present plight. Their experience of alienation is unmistakable:

> When you work day in and day out at a scientifically managed job like typing or packing ping-pong paddles, you certainly feel like something is missing. But the constriction, the listlessness, the absence of that spark comes to seem like a natural part of your character. . . . The present system would seem even more alien to human nature were it not so pervasive. Who would imagine that the biological jack-of-all trades [humankind]—the renaissance animal—would have to work like a squirrel, a woodpecker, an earthworm?[21]

Work is endured, but not enjoyed. Life's meaning and value are found apart from work. Work is more often alienating than fulfilling.

We express our humanity as we create or act upon material reality, but in alienation, this internal relation between the worker and what she or he makes disappears.[22] Labor is broken down into calculable elements, leading to a fragmentation of the human subject, who becomes a mechanized part of a process that is preexisting and self-sufficient—a closed system to which the worker must conform. Productive activity becomes objective and external. The self is controlled, dominated, denied, rather than affirmed. Workers only feel at home outside of their work. They feel separated from the products of their labor.

The life that workers have put into the material now belongs to the object, which has greater value than the workers. What is produced becomes a power confronting those who produced it. The means of production employ the worker, or, in our day, threaten to unemploy the laborer. Workers are made to feel guilty for producing products that cost more, are outpriced in the competitive global market, and consequently result in additional job cutbacks. The more workers produce, the more they feel under this domination. Even farmers, long seen as a refuge from alienated labor, are being dominated by what they have produced.

Alienated from their life activities and products, human beings become alienated from one another. For some workers this alienation is from the boss or manager. But this alienation from others is also apparent in that persons are valued insofar as they are necessary for the exchange of things, according to how much they are worth in dollar-and-cents terms. The relationship between persons tends to be materially based under capitalism. The material value of exchange becomes the basis for community. Community becomes important only as a means to the survival of the individual and his or her family. Human potential becomes identified with the individual's capacity to sell labor power. In these terms, those in unpaid work, especially homemakers or the unemployed, are not valued.

The objects produced and the workers themselves come to be viewed as commodities, valued by their price or wage. This is *reification*. Historical relations, that is, what human beings have created, take on the appearance of natural facts, and thus acquire an ontological status.[23] "That's the way it is!" is working people's typical acknowledgment of reification. Human beings become passive subjects of their own alienated existence, rather than historical agents. Survival depends on adapting to a reality that confronts one as absolute and overpowering. Economic and social forces become blind, "natural" forces to which one must adjust. "You gotta go along with it!" is the typical attitude of resignation. "That's the way it is" acquires its own rationality. "In every aspect of daily life in which the individual worker imagines himself [*sic*] to be subject of his own life, he finds this to be an illusion that is destroyed by the immediacy of his existence."[24] The world appears in fixed, absolute terms. Obedience to authority, conventionalism, and a rigid acceptance of the status quo prevail. Human institutions are seen as products and symbols of some normal, external, and superordinate authority one must conform to, rather than as human in origin and character.

Those doing manual work rather than mental may be less vulnerable to reification than those in the primary labor market who are part of rationalized bureaucracies. Being able to "turn off" one's brain while working may be an important means of escaping total reification. But as working people move upward into more intellectually demanding jobs, thereby capturing society's respect, the work often feels less "real," and workers lose respect for themselves.[25] For many, manual work still seems to have more dignity. It may be alienating or demeaning, but producing something with one's hands feels more like work.

Richard Sennett and Jonathan Cobb describe the sepa-ration that arises in working-class men between the exercise of personal power—doing a good job to get ahead, and the real self—revealed to family and friends, without having to prove oneself. Workers tend to construct reality so that their real self is cut off from the performing worker, free from having to compete and thus protected from the wounds of class society. If they gain approval from those above them by doing a good job at work, they worry about no longer being "one of the guys," thus losing the real dignity and respect that comes from their buddies without being earned. Occupational achievements, competence, and power are kept external so the worker can avoid being seen as an institutional person, and being socially isolated from co-workers.

Thus, the passive rather than the active voice is used. Rather than "I did" or "I earned," the common expression is "they gave me" or "it was done for me." Not claiming that "I" did or achieved it serves as a protective defense as to why some make it and most do not. "I'll do the work but 'I' won't be there doing it" provides ontological security in the face of the wounding so common in their experience.[26] The self is acted upon rather than being the agent of historical activity. Human responsibility is replaced by functional responsi-bility—in order to "fit into how things are." Action or power is kept separate from feeling or love.

This splitting of the private self known to family and friends from the public self of the workplace is characteris-tic of capitalist society, and is a central obstacle to the emer-gence of critical consciousness and transformative praxis. The private realm of home and family is seen as the realm free from the domination and alienation one experiences in "the world," especially in the workplace. But is it really that free?

Working People's Quest for Freedom

American working people are strongly opposed to the possibility of being dominated or determined by outside forces. The spirit of the American dream conditions human beings to make every effort to escape from domination or deny that they are dominated. "[T]he underlying and fundamental need of human beings for a deeper respect, for a loving community, and for the opportunity to actualize their deepest human capacities continues to assert itself and will not be silenced."[27] Workers hope that these needs will be met through the institutions of private life—home and family, and the values and activities engendered therein.

The sacred place for most working people is their own home. It is an island of freedom in a world of control by others—the source of one's pride and expression of one's real identity. The big ostentatious investments, which may take years to pay off, are carefully protected—for example, the velvet couch is covered with stiff plastic. The center of the home is likely to be a big color television.

Family, including the extended family, is considered all-important. One moves away from family only when forced to because of the lack of employment. Kinship patterns tend to be far tighter than for those who are upwardly mobile.[28]

The home is where the working-class man tends to feel he can exercise his authority. He expects to receive the respect here that he lacks in the world. As one man commented regarding his grown son: "This is my house, he has the option to go and live on his own if he wants. But as long as he's under my roof, he has to abide by my rules."[29] The man's wife and children are perceived as his private property, the objects of his control and manipulation. Thus, it is no surprise that when workplace frustrations are brought home, domestic violence is a real possibility.

Working-class wives value husbands who are steady workers, who do not drink too much, and who do not hit them.[30] Emotional values of intimacy, sharing, and communication have been less important than for couples of a higher class. "He" typically has been "her" means of access to the American dream. The man understands that his work is what will achieve the American dream for his family. The dream is more derivative for the woman.[31] Her labor has had less effect on the realization of the dream. Instead, she may participate in the dream by depending upon and taking care of her husband and children—her means of upward mobility. Her work has been creating and maintaining relationships, and countering the demeaning effects of the wage economy through her nurturing and caring.

A working-class woman who works outside the home tends to increase her authority in marriage, much to the chagrin of her husband. However, her entry into the job market is usually not due to choice but to economic necessity—if her husband experiences downward mobility or unemployment, or because she has no husband. Because a woman has been seen first as a "woman" only secondarily as a "worker," her job status in the labor market has been characteristically low. Therefore, a woman most often finds employment in the secondary labor market of low wages, benefits, and security. She is subordinated in the home because she is a woman, and in the workplace because she is a woman, and hence employed in the secondary labor market.

During the past two decades, an increasing proportion of younger women, including those who are working-class, have begun aspiring to realize the American dream on their own.[32] Yet for many the dream continues to be in relationship to a man. It is impelled by a vision of the good life, an eschatological horizon that never seems to be reached by husband or wife. The good life consists in having an ever-greater measure of goods and pleasures in order to be happy.

This quest for "salvation" (the hoped-for "good life") operates, with variations, according to the following cycle: the husband works hard to earn the good life. The value of working is found through purchasing consumer goods and other amenities, the signs of one's achievements. Greater conspicuous consumption provides greater psychological compensation for the rote meaninglessness of the job. Outward trappings provide the sense of identity that is desperately needed in a class society. By buying on credit until the bills mount up, one continues consuming to soothe one's wounded ego. The more one buys, the deeper one falls into bondage to the job in order to pay the bills. Eventually one reaches the point of taking on a second job, or having one's spouse get a job. Either option results in guilt, which is internalized. The second job leaves less time for the all-important family, with whom to enjoy the good life. Just as one has made enough to buy that boat to enjoy on weekends, one is forced to work weekends in order to pay it off. If a man's wife gets a job, it may also contribute to his sense of failure—this time the failure to provide for his family.

If the woman is the breadwinner, the cycle of bills compounds because of her lower income. As a woman alone, she may feel additional pressure to make it. However, a working woman's identity and sense of worth have been less likely to be tied to a paying job than it is for a man. The job has been only part of her identity. A career is only part of her work identity, the other part being her work at home. If she is married, the significance of her work is considered less crucial. She is seen as working temporarily to help pay the bills.

The cycle remains unquestioned. In this society it is considered the only game to play. Therefore, the man continues to recommit himself to faith in his ability to make it—and prove his manhood—if he keeps trying harder and repeating the cycle. Thus, the rules of the game are reinforced, his bondage to "the way things are" is increased, his frustration, anxiety, and guilt become more individualized, and "salvation"—the hoped-for good life—continues to elude his grasp.

If the chances of moving upward or achieving the good life appear slim, one will do anything to ensure that one's children will make it.

Equipping the children for upward mobility is a top priority. And yet, the typical child-rearing values of the working class condition children to become like their parents. Conformity to external standards or authorities is emphasized, in contrast to an emphasis on self-direction and critical questioning.[33] Constraint is important in maintaining order and obedience. Knowing *that* something is wrong is considered far more important than knowing *why* it is wrong. The emphasis on external conformity is crucial in preparing children for jobs in which conformity to rules and authority will be necessary. The assumption is that conformity to external authority will enable children to move upward. Yet the parents' own experience, as well as global developments in capitalism, cast doubt on the likelihood of that outcome.

There is ambivalence in what working-class parents want their children to become. Parents see their own lives serving as warnings rather than as examples: "Don't become like us—better yourself." They are determined that their children will be different. Consequently, they do what is in their power: they sacrifice for their children.[34]

The sacrifice is one of the few expressions of freedom and control available to working people. They hope their children will achieve a better future, and thus "redeem" the sacrifices they are making. But what happens to the meaning of this sacrifice? Either children let parents down, so that the sacrificer feels betrayed, or if children do achieve upward mobility, they seem to pull rank. They acquire different values and life styles, move away psychologically if not geographically, and often develop a disdain for their parents' reality. As a result, parents feel betrayed in an even deeper sense. Their children no longer feel like extensions of themselves, through whom they might experience vicarious satisfaction and the redemption of their sacrifice.

The Dream Is Betrayed

Even more jarring can be the sense of betrayal when one loses one's job despite one's best efforts. The cycle in endless pursuit of "the good life" is cast into crisis when the job market shifts and unemployment rises. Some workers find themselves thrown off the cycle's treadmill, cast into a camp with the underclass, those others who have not made it. Those who counsel the unemployed have noted a process of grieving that is strikingly similar to that occurring at the death of a loved one. The goal of their striving collapses. Anomie sets in. The promise of the good life explodes in their faces.

There is an opportunity to question the rule or ideology by which the American dream operates, but in most cases that does not occur. Instead, working people wait out the crisis, try to get by day by day until other jobs come along, enabling them to step back into the cycle.

Working people do not experience themselves as active historical subjects in the public world. The real self is confined to the private realm of family and friends, feeling powerless to change the wider realities that impact their lives. Unemployment is something done to them and over which they have no control. It contradicts the ideology of individual effort on which working people have staked their lives.

Suddenly the realization dawns that the individual strivings by which one seeks to make something of oneself are to no avail. "Effortocracy" has failed to save one's job or one's dignity. Instead, it has set one in deeper bondage to the structures that control and distort human life.

Therefore, the challenge is twofold: (1) How can working people break out of this enslaving cycle of disappointed, bankrupt promises? (2) How can they regain a sense of themselves as active historical subjects in the world? It is a pervasively spiritual-theological challenge.

3

Religion and the Realities of Class

Working People's Religiosity

Working people's lives are so enmeshed in a web of forces that dominate or exercise control over them that their religious yearning is for freedom, dignity, and a sense of worth. They want to be somebody amid the forces that treat them as nobody. Workers' religiosity is characterized by an immediately felt need for salvation from the social and economic forces upon which they are dependent. The realm of religion is viewed as being free from society's domination.

The black spiritual, "Oh, Freedom," was the favorite song of many of the white working-class members of a parish I pastored. Even though many resented the blacks who were moving into their neighborhood, and had little appreciation for black culture, this song from a tradition that has long sustained oppressed people spoke to their deep religious yearnings as white working people. They also appreciated my practice of naming each person as I served communion at the altar rail. Song, prayer, and ritual are needed to express who and whose one is as a person in the face of situations that deny such expression.

In this sense, religion is not first of all an "opiate," as the Marxist characterization would allege, but an arena of protest against the wounds inflicted in a class society, or as Marx himself put it, "the sigh of the oppressed creature." It is a protest against the alienation of human nature that occurs through industrial capitalism. The popular religion of working people is a form of *social expression*. It is not necessarily found in their church language but in songs and other expressions of popular culture, which are permeated with working people's psalmic laments. Songs popular among the working class describe how one tries to get through the day, comes home pretending that it is not so bad, "and when the morning light comes streaming in you'll get up and do it again." Working-class taverns are more likely to be respected sanctuaries for these expressions than are organized churches.

The popular religion manifest in such expressions is likely to be (1) materialistic, arising out of a concrete historical situation, rather than idealistic, (2) based on "common sense," (3) rooted in feelings rather than intellect, (4) focused on cyclical, sometimes magical rituals, and (5) imbued with a politico-social conservatism.[1] Prayer and devotional life as well as creeds stating what to believe are typically more important in the religious life of working people than for those of higher classes.

The tenets of Christianity, although believed sincerely, do not constitute (especially for working-class men) their primary cosmology, that is, that set of beliefs considered true and relevant for their life in the world.[2] Although religious yearnings arise out of one's plight in the world, religion is usually viewed as compartmentalized from one's life in the world. It offers the promise of an eventual escape. Getting to heaven, where one receives one's compensation, becomes the means of escape from domination.

Their Encounter with the Church

The religious yearnings of working people do not necessarily translate into church attendance. Many are deeply suspicious of highly trained clerics ("phony preachers") and of the gap between belief and action among churchgoers ("the church is full of hypocrites"). Church is another arena where many working people feel looked down on for how they dress, talk, or live. This is especially true of "hard livers," particularly if the denomination or congregation is characterized by an upper-middle-class ethos. In such congregations workers are likely to sit near the back and try to remain inconspicuous.

Although working people's religious preferences are often thought of as sectlike, they affiliate in sizable numbers with most denominations. Lutherans, Baptists, and Methodists, followed by the sects, Roman Catholics, Episcopalians, and Presbyterians, are those with high percentages of working-class members.[3] Working people attend as regularly as those of higher classes, or (in the case of many men) hardly attend at all.

The respectable, deferential workers are most active in churches. Church attendance demonstrates that one is respectable, responsible, and proper—a faithful adherent to the promise of the American dream. Affiliating with a higher-class church helps to convince working people themselves and others that they are moving upward, toward the eschaton of the good life and heaven (which become operationally equivalent). Consequently, when workers lose their jobs or farmers lose their farms, they typically stop going to church. The notion that upward mobility is a sign of God's blessing is so deeply ingrained, and the message of the church has become so closely identified with the American dream, that it is hard to imagine that the church has much to offer when the dream has been betrayed.

Classism and the Church. The gospel message may be one of freedom and salvation—a constant reminder that our different social positions do not matter because we are "one in Christ"—but most churches experience the same classism operating in the rest of society.

In most mainline churches this first occurs through the prevalent language. Language reflects the social structure of a given society, and how persons understand themselves in that society. Working people often find the language used in church and worship overbearing. They are afraid to speak for fear of embarrassment. Everyone else seems to know so much. You can't understand the preacher's fancy words. In the same way that male-dominant language and imagery tend to overlook the experience of women, language can exclude working people from the social reality of those of a higher stratum. One way this occurs is through the elevation of Latin-derived over Anglo-Saxon-derived words.[4]

Class bias is communicated through the elaborate code that seminarians must master in order to become professional clergy. This is often at the cost of leaving behind the language that might better communicate with working-class parishioners. The formal language of those with higher education is nuanced, reflective, analytical, and abstract. It is able to cope with ambiguities, to question what is, and tends to focus on the "I" of the enlightened self. It is important for social transformation, but can be used to put down working people rather than transform their situation in the world.

In contrast, the language of working people tends to be of a restricted code, with direct, simple statements that are concrete, emotive, and often take the form of commands. Obedience to rules is engendered, without questioning why. What is *not* said is often more important than what is said. The communal "we" is valued over the personal "I." The role system is more closed, novel meanings are discouraged, and the conceptual order is limited. Authority patterns are clear-cut and explicit, with unambiguous boundaries—especially in matters of morality. A given behavior is either right or wrong. The set form of social relations is reinforced through language and accepted as rational, natural, inevitable. It is difficult to question the injustice of a given social arrangement, which is why such appeals often fall on deaf ears. One's place in the social order is precarious enough, such that questioning it and risking one's security is not an inviting prospect.

In many mainline churches working people do not find the personal, feeling-level piety that they desire (except in some of the hymns that clergy grudgingly "let" the people sing). Instead they find a formal liturgical style and an impersonal, ethical, cosmic, or absolutely transcendent God that Max Weber found to be alien to workers.[5] It is not that they are unaccustomed to hierarchical structures of authority or "good order," and hence such worship styles. In fact, many deferential working people prefer such styles. But such styles may cut off the indigenous religious expressions of workers who desire to be free from the structures of authority that the church makes legitimate. In that sense, the church becomes an "opiate," and a vehicle of *social control* rather than social expression for the working class.

This also occurs through the organization and decision-making processes of the church. If members of a professional/managerial status are willing and able to serve in church leadership positions, working people may be hesitant or unwilling to do so. For example, the slate of officers and committee members elected at Lutheran church-wide conventions rarely includes anyone in a working-class occupation who is not at least married to a professional. The church's decision making may be more inclusive of women or persons of color, but not of working people. This exclusion is not intentional. It is due to the professional/managerial class bias inherent in much of the institutional church's corporate, bureaucratic style of operation. The church has become another corporation with a set of experts telling people what to believe or do. Decisions are made in such a way that working people feel their voice and perspectives do not matter.

The church may talk about the ministry of the laity, but the focus of churches usually is on the vocation of those in professional/managerial occupations. Luther's doctrine of vocation intended to give dignity to even the most demeaning jobs. However, it is difficult for working people to discern how to serve God through their work other than by being faithful to their boss and hence to God.

In the local congregation the property committee (work of the hands) is a less threatening place to serve than the budget committee (work of the mind). The working class prefers church council meetings that are run more like family gatherings—the highpoint being the socializing that occurs during the refreshment break. Professional/managerial persons may view such meetings as time-consuming and inefficient.

Church as Community. Tex Sample identifies the important communal function that church fulfills for blue-collar persons.[6] The church is a "family," a *Gemeinschaft* of primary social relations, rather than an association of secondary social relations. The nurturing of bonds with one another is more important than making a decision or accomplishing a task. The yearning for community and a sense of solidarity with one another is crucial in a society where persons often feel alienated and unwhole. Developing communal bonds between members needs to be honored in the church, even if the supposed "real business" of the church does not get done.

Some of that "real business" involves working to see that a congregation has a future. The church is a community where one's upward mobility is legitimated and celebrated, not so much as a sign of individual achievement but as a sign of God's blessings. Even if one experiences betrayal of the American dream, the hope is kept alive of passing on to one's children the dream as it is embedded in the church. That hope too is often disappointed, sometimes because the children sense how insidiously the church and the dream are intertwined. The church is an auxiliary of the dream, which is where Americans' real "faith" may be lodged.

The Ideology of Classism

The religious yearnings of working people are usually not addressed in the church in ways that can transform their world. The heart of the gospel may be an important counter to classism, but the more powerful message is how class values are perpetuated in the church's institutional life. The church becomes another area where working people experience the pain of class.

The religious yearnings are usually indistinguishable from the preferred religious expressions, but these tend to serve an ideological function within a class society. When people experience sociopsychological strain, but lack the cultural or theological resources to make sense of it, they turn to the predominant ideology. This becomes the sieve through which the religious tradition is sifted. The sieve of the American dream results in religious expressions that are typically privatized and removed from history, and that legitimize the present structures of society. For example, Jesus Christ's activity is understood as saving individuals from history, in a way that overlooks the sociality and historicity of human existence in the world.

47

It is difficult if not impossible for the church professional to get at these yearnings apart from the ideology of the American dream, which the professional is seen as upholding, as the "manager" of the "company." Working people are likely to cling to a hierarchical, authoritarian, fixed social order, which ironically has been the source of their victimization. They do so because of the precariousness of life in an age when the dream is being betrayed all around them. They cling to a privatized religion removed from their worldly struggles because in their private realm they can be themselves, the real self or "soul" can live and the wounds be forgotten. They adopt the upwardly mobile values and religious orientation of those above them because of their tenacious belief that in the end the dream will "save" them. In other words, their religious expressions have been colonized or become captive to the dynamics of domination from which they seek salvation.

What is selectively *heard* in the church's preaching and teaching correlates with how working people perceive and interpret reality. We hear and put together the meaning of what is being said from out of our own life experience.

A Working-Class View of God. I thought I was preaching the gospel to my parishioners, but discovered that my sermons were being filtered through a moralistic understanding of religion, centered on the Ten Commandments. Working people have been conditioned to pay particular attention to authoritative directions. Obedience and submission to laws and authorities and individual expressions of piety and morality enable them to "get by" in the world. Consequently, that is what they tend to latch onto in their understanding of the Christian faith. If one fears, loves, and trusts God so as not to curse or swear; if one goes to church on Sundays, obeys one's parents, does not murder anyone or cheat on one's spouse, one is better than some people. One may even feel more moral than one's superiors!

God becomes the paradigm of a distant, hierarchical authority; the legitimation of the authority that is structured into all other orders of life; an authority who calls for a submissiveness that serves the interest of a class-structured society. As Luther puts it, we are not to "despise or anger our parents and others in authority, but respect, obey, love and serve them."[7] Our respect and obedience toward such authorities do not depend on what they do or what they are like as persons. The God-instituted office that they occupy is sufficient to deserve our respect. As an old hymn puts it,

> The rich man in his castle,
> The poor man at his gate,
> God made them high or lowly,
> And ordered their estate.

Subordinates are forbidden to get angry over their situation, but those in positions of authority are to exercise their anger as an expression of God's anger. God puts us in our place and intends for us to live in harmony with our neighbors, regardless of their material advantage over us. These kinds of understandings, whether or not they are true to what was intended, help keep in place the structures and ideology of classism.

A Lutheran Church in America study of a sampling of parishioners who attend adult forums, and thus are likely to be more informed regarding the meaning of the faith, surfaced some interesting responses from working people (especially laborers). They relied to a greater extent on external religious authority and placed importance on merely believing that something is so. They were more likely to have an unquestioned acceptance of a God who is in control, who at times even works against their interests. Only 22 percent felt that "God has let me make the decisions." Two-thirds strongly supported the statement, "Most of us have worked hard for what we have and we resent it being taken away."[8]

The pastoral dilemma is trying to honor what is behind the religious expressions with which working people identify, while at the same time trying to counter the ideological purposes to which such expressions can become captive. The latter task becomes necessary as the ideology and its tenets become the active religion or "god" in people's lives, making the biblical God a captive of the dream.

"Faith" in the American Dream

An ideology is a system of interacting symbols or pattern of interworking meanings that functions like a religion. A religion, according to Clifford Geertz, is a system of symbols that acts to establish powerful, pervasive, and long-lasting moods and motivations in people by (1) formulating conceptions of a general order of existence, and (2) clothing these conceptions with such an aura of factuality that the moods and motivations seem uniquely realistic.[9] The ideology of the American dream has become a religion in this sense.

"Faith" is lodged in the dream's promise of freedom, equality, and happiness for all, as epitomized in the good life. Yearning for the good life becomes the central religious aspiration, reinforced by images of the good life preached by television evangelists. Local parishioners ask their pastors, "Why can't you tell us what heaven's like in the way Falwell does?" The specifications of the good life are always changing, especially in the direction of a bigger and better trajectory that continually eludes satisfaction. Growth and upward mobility are hallmarks of this faith. Sacrifices are either blotted out or reinterpreted to make the gains seem worth it. "The afterlife in which Americans receive their just rewards for the virtue of hard work is found at the shopping center. . . . Hunger for more is promoted as a moral imperative."[10] Shopping centers (typically laid out in a cross design, with the ends anchored by big department stores) become the sanctuaries where adherents of this religion flock. Cracks or contradictions that challenge the validity of this basic faith are quickly rationalized or covered over with the assurance that we are back on the road of continuing growth. Growth or highest possible profit becomes the prevailing discourse of power, the absolute for which persons and communities are sacrificed.

Even though many may be questioning the validity of the American dream, it still is alive and well for the vast majority of Americans.[11] Seventeen percent of Midwesterners (where so many plants have closed and farms have been lost) and only 8 percent of Westerners acknowledge that the dream no longer has meaning. To challenge the hegemony of the dream is to risk being declared a traitor or heretic of its basic faith system. The irony is that working people, desperate for a sense of self-worth and dignity, often place even more faith in its promise. The emptiness of the promise may be more apparent to persons in a higher stratum who have acquired more of the dream's material trappings. Those who "have" generate ever-expanding criteria of what constitutes the dream, so that workers, although they may have made visible progress, continue to fall short of the good life.

People do not talk about the good life apart from the plan or ideological tenets by which they hope to acquire it, which is an interpretation of what this faith is, namely, something that the individual acquires. It is difficult if not impossible to challenge these tenets from within a faith system that undergirds and legitimates them. For example, one cannot discern what is wrong with an ideology of individualism from within a faith system in which the individual acquiring the

51

good life is the basic hope of salvation. It becomes a closed, self-perpetuating totality. To rise up against its central values is to rise up against what seems like "God."

Thus, although the American dream is not inherently idolatrous, it becomes godlike in its rule over people's lives when it becomes the focus of one's "faith" or ultimate meaning. In idolatry people seek salvation through political and religious submission to powers of domination.[12] The idol becomes a veil of illusion, preventing people from seeing alternative ways of being or living. In that sense, it closes off historicity. What is primary is not idolatry's effect on God but its effect on us. Whenever anyone or anything becomes god for us, it becomes an unquestioned absolute and reigns over us regardless of the human or historical consequences. This is idolatry.

Individualism, victimization, and privatization interrelate and function as a resilient "trinity" reigning over working people's lives. Individualism puts the burden on the individual to make a difference, to succeed. Individual effort, know-how, or luck determines whether one acquires the good life. One is in a competitive rather than cooperative relationship with others, such that one will not let on if one is failing.

Yet the pervasive experience of working people is that despite their works and hopes they have not acquired the fruits of this individualism. Consequently, there is a temporary shift from their individualistic worldview to a worldview of victimization: "it was done to me." The active idealism at the core of American individualism is transfigured into a stance of passivity, resignation, or inevitability: "there's nothing that I as an individual can do about the forces out there." Conservative political rhetoric builds upon this worldview, with the promise that the good life can be achieved once again if restraints on individual liberty are stripped away.

Any potential for solidarity with other victims, for questioning social structures, and for empowerment is turned back into an individualistic rejuvenation of the American dream.

Yet because victimization feels so inevitable—there is nothing one can do to effect the social matrix of one's life—one concentrates instead on the private arena of life to seek fulfillment, happiness, meaning, and some semblance of the good life. The result is an intensified privatization of life, aided by an increasingly individualized, spiritualized, ahistorical theology, cut off from the public realities or structures that shape the private expressions of working people's lives.

A contradiction arises. What workers have lost through victimization has not been regained through privatization, because through this process they have been rendered impotent to affect the socio-economic-political factors that determine their reality.

Thus, the three dynamics—individualism, victimization, and privatization—reinforce one another, as well as mask the contradictions of the idolatry that the three together perpetuate, and that tragically holds working people in bondage when the dream betrays them.

How can this situation be redeemed?

4

Theological Perspectives for Addressing Class Realities

The Theological Challenge

If the threefold entrapment of individualism, victimization, and privatization perpetuates what has become an idolatrous situation—as epitomized in American capitalist society—then the power that constitutes that idol needs to be recognized as human not divine, as historical not necessary, as changeable not inevitable.

Working people must be able to express their genuine needs and claim their social context as the space for satisfying those needs. God views human beings and their needs as important. Faith in this biblical God, in whose image we are created, liberates us from the cultural-economic-political idol in whose image we have been falsely recreated.[1]

The totality of any system's grip on us can be critiqued only by means of a more pervasive claim on our lives. God's claim is that we might become more fully human, subjects in history, actualizing the freedom that God intends for us. Such a "faith lived in the struggle for material, corporal life is compelled to seek the illegitimating of the gods that produce and inhabit systems of oppression."[2]

How can those who are characteristically working class engage in a theological project of denouncing what is and annunciating what might be, of challenging and transforming, of addressing the objective as well as the subjective realities of their situation? How can they become active historical subjects in the face of the domination they experience? How might they reflect theologically on their experience rather than being told what to believe by clergy and others in authority?

Challenging Idolatry. Idolatry must be exposed. However, this is a complex theological task. Simply denouncing the obvious idols of profit and competitiveness, which underlie the dilemma that workers face, is as likely to lead to a separatist, otherworldly disengagement from social realities as it is to transformative change. Most workers feel that disassociating from these powers is impossible due to basic survival needs. This reinforces the sharp split of the private religious self from the public self, who cannot realistically expect to extricate him- or herself from complicity with such idols.

Naming the idol that dominates, without addressing the subjective sense of alienation and apathy is not likely to change the reality of most working people. The idol's hold over people's lives must be loosened. This begins when their experience becomes the basis for critiquing the values associated with the idol. Values of equality are espoused but the reality is one of increasing inequality. Workers who have cast their hopes on becoming successes are finding themselves betrayed—living contradictions of American capitalist culture. The discrepancies between the promise and the reality in their lives are more apparent than for those of a higher class. Disparities between society's claims and its concrete relations of power become more evident.

The contradictions begin to expose the ideology of the American dream that upholds the idolatry. The dream promises the good life, but one is led into bondage by submitting to that promise. Contradictions inherent in a system culminate in a turning point that demands resolution, in a crisis that demands a conversion—not a turning away from but toward an address of those realities. Conversion is first and foremost a theological occurrence, but it is lived out through sociopolitical engagement.

In Search of a Transforming Theology. Theology is reflection on social and personal reality in light of the Christian faith. Theology that can transform workers' reality, that exposes and moves beyond individualism-privatization-victimization, must be transcendent (not captive to the ideology and system defining people's reality) as well as immanent (congruent with their experience). It must be able to address the objective determinants as well as the subjective experience of workers.

The prophetic task of knocking down the idols must be linked with the pastoral task of responding to the hopes and fears that the idol addresses. The idol promises security and a future, and has provided such for many. This is why it seems so believable, even when it betrays its loyal adherents. The pastoral-theological challenge is to recognize the sufferings, betrayals, and contradictions rather than cover them over.

In addition to this ideological critique, the process of exposing the idols involves reenvisioning the human subject. A shift is needed from an individualistic to a more social understanding of human beings, from a sense of victimization to one of empowerment, from a privatization to a politicization of personal and public life. Theological perspectives are needed that can convert working people from being passive objects of godlike powers to active subjects engaged in a faith-constituted *praxis*, that is, participatory action that increases human freedom in society.

This chapter explores some theological perspectives that provide the groundwork for a movement that transforms class realities.

The Emergence of Modern Theology

Analysis of the working-class dilemma presupposes a commitment to the modern theological project, which is marked by the quest for the authenticity of the subject. In premodern theology, God determines the parameters and occurrences of history. Human life becomes a temporal passage full of pain and suffering, which one endures in anticipation of the fulfillment that lies beyond this world. Two planes are operative: an eternal, unchanging realm of God and the tragic sphere of human life governed by fate. This position is still current among many of the fundamentalist religious groups with whom workers identify.

In the modern worldview, human beings have become progressively more autonomous, with the power to determine the conditions of their lives. The promise of a free market economy is that it can organize and control millions of human beings without an external authority, be it human or divine. The world is shaped by human decisions and actions. It becomes rational, functional, historical. Society becomes separate from religion. Thus, modern theology attempts to address this split and reinterpret Christian theology in terms credible to modern persons. For example, faith becomes linked with freedom, which constitutes human existence.

Nineteenth-century liberal theology accommodated religion to modern times and put its faith in historical progress. When historical optimism broke down early in this century, various forms of neoorthodox theology arose, which insisted that the meaning of life and the experience of God had to come from beyond or outside of history. Faith needed to be secured outside the process of history—through revelation. History was taken seriously, but neoorthodoxy worked through history to get beyond history, and to assure the non-identity of Christianity with the world.[3]

The theologian Paul Tillich dealt with this modern dilemma. Tillich saw the modern spirit of finite self-sufficiency epitomized in the Weimar Republic of the 1920s. Society's hope and purpose were focused on the es-tablishment of human control over nature and mind, thereby exalting the finite into an absolute.[4] Capitalist society had become a civilization based on this faith in self-sufficiency, which became a central theological problem for Tillich. Re-ligion was becoming increasingly secularized, and thus cap-tive to current economic and political forces. Christianity and modern society had become so identified with each other that the former had lost its possibility of prophetic critique.[5]

This description applies to much of the religion practiced in contemporary American culture. Religion has become a tool enabling individuals to succeed in material terms, with the invocation of God to bless such efforts. If or when one becomes affluent, one claims to have been blessed by God. The social dimension of one's Christian faith tends to be ex-hausted in terms of helping others less fortunate, who are perceived as being less blessed by God. Religion's appeal is in the personal fulfillment it promises: to make individuals feel better or to feel happier.

Tillich describes the developments that bring society to this point. In what he calls the "sacramental spiritual situa-tion," the relation of persons had been determined directly by the consecrated cultic community. Reality had a sacramental immediacy. This was typical of the medieval culture that served as the backdrop for Martin Luther's theology. With the Enlightenment-inspired emphasis on the emancipation of persons, the sacred connections to power disappear, as does the living import of community. Communities that form are based on common economic interests. Subjective forces break into a situation that is now rooted in the liberal notion of free personalities.

Thus, Tillich juxtaposed "belief-ful realism" over against this finite self-sufficiency. Material reality is accepted as given, without idealizing or spiritualizing it. Yet belief-ful realism is a stance in tension with the givens, enabling the present to be analyzed in light of the eternal, whose meaning is present in the historical particulars. Belief-ful realism expressed Tillich's hope for a social and economic life in which the "demonic" spirit of capitalism is overcome. The demonic is manifest in the way that the destruction of spiritual freedom and creative power holds classes in bondage and generates apathy.[6] The theological task is to restore that freedom and power.

All references to the power of our origin are abolished when we are treated like objects. People become profane, rational economic commodities over which the subjective will to power prevails. The vital center of being—Tillich calls it the "power of origin"—is what protects human beings from totally succumbing to the spirit of domination and loss of historical consciousness. With a new sense of who they are and where they have come from, workers begin to reinterpret what has happened in their lives with new sociohistorical understandings.

This power of origin shapes Tillich's socialist vision, which is based on the premise that each individual be treated according to his or her destiny or power of origin. It is a religious vision of prophetism on the soil of an autonomous, self-sufficient world.[7] Tillich searched for a means of emancipation from the limitless drive of a rational liberal industrial economy. Key to this is emergence of an eros-relation to things, which is what *theonomy* denotes. Under theonomy, social forms are filled with the importance of the Unconditional. Socio-economic-political matters become theological matters.

This sociopolitical theology was no longer evident by the time Tillich wrote his *Systematic Theology*. His goal then was to overcome the split between modern consciousness and religious faith, thereby placing himself in the center of twentieth-century modern theology. He saw reason and revelation as interrelated, not in conflict, with ontological reason as the underpinning for his theological system. His focus was on humanistically educated skeptics, rather than on working-class persons. His pessimism regarding the possibility of theory and practice being joined in history led him away from a focus on praxis and toward preoccupation with theology as theory.

Liberation Theology

During the past two decades liberation theologians have built upon the modern theological project (modern working people should be active subjects rather than passive objects) while also departing from it at significant points. They presuppose historical consciousness (human beings are responsible for what happens), the centrality of freedom, and the need to correlate the historical situation with Christian symbols. All knowledge of God is mediated through the world; human history is the arena of God's activity.

However, liberation theologians are sometimes referred to as postmodern because of their outrage over the sinister distortions of modern times, namely, that "the labors of freedom have produced the chains of oppression."[8] The freedom exercised by autonomous human subjects has also resulted in control and domination. Those who have been subjugated are the concern of liberation theologies. If modern theology's concern has been with the *cultured despisers* of religion, liberation theology's focus is on the *culturally despised*—those oppressed because of class, sex, or race, who have been dominated and treated as nonpersons by Enlightenment-inspired subjects.

Rebecca Chopp summarizes the divergences:

> Latin American liberation theology continues modern theology's concern for the subject, the representation of freedom by Christianity, and the experience of faith in history but, in a radical reformulation, defines the subject as the poor, reinterprets freedom to include political self-determination, and envisions history as the arena for both liberation and redemption.[9]

The crisis of meaning shifts to this worldly social-historical existence. The social nature of human existence, and hence the connections with those who are treated as nonpersons, becomes a theological problem. We come to know God through the suffering victims of history, for whom God exercises a preferential option. Salvation has meaning in historical terms as liberation, which becomes meaningful through faith-constituted praxis. Faith becomes an existential mode of human freedom that embraces knowledge and action. It is a lived reality. The point is not to understand faith differently, but to allow a new faith to spring from a new praxis, a praxis that attempts to transform the world. Theology becomes reflection on this praxis—interpreting, guiding, and critiquing it.

Political Theology

The affinities between liberation and political theologies are far greater than their differences, which are mainly due to context and audience. Whereas liberation theology's focus is on the poor, political theology's focus tends to be on middle-class, bourgeois society and those who seek to identify with that ethos. Liberation theology arose in response to oppression and injustice in Latin America; political theology emerged over two decades ago as a reaction to secularized German society. Liberation theology critiques the developments that shaped Latin American realities; political theology critiques the privatization that is endemic in Western capitalist society. The impetus of liberation theology is on transforming the world; political theologians' emphasis is on ideological critique of society, bringing about greater solidarity with the suffering victims of the world.

The context out of which German political theology arises is closer to that of North American workers than the Latin American context of liberation theology. To cope or survive in this society, American workers have had to assume modern consciousness, mythos, and ethos, but they have been dominated objects rather than participatory subjects in this consciousness. The workers' sociopolitical awareness of their exclusion or victimization emerges when they connect their experience with the suffering of others who have been more dramatically excluded, for example, oppressed Latin American peasants. And yet ideological blocks work against that. North American workers are caught in the cross fire between modern and postmodern developments. The illusion is that they are free subjects, but their experience is that of being victims. As many lament, "I've worked hard, but now I'm out of a job."

Political theology is not a theology of politics but a hermeneutic of the relationship of religion and society. It critiques the ideology in a society or system from the perspective of social-political understandings of Christian faith. Like liberation theology, it is a way of understanding the close interrelationship between theory and praxis. Reality is interpreted from the horizon of historical praxis rather than from a fixed ontological or ahistorical horizon. Faith is enacted in society. Transformative praxis discloses truth. Such theology should not be used to justify certain political options, but to critique such justifications. It does not solve political or social questions but interrupts any system that tries to become absolute or godlike. It reappropriates the social character of biblical images, using them for a continual critique of the socio-political-economic order.

Political theology arose as a critique of the inadequacy of existential theology, and to correct the privatization that the latter reinforced. Theology had become so focused on individual decision apart from the sociopolitical context that the social, public, political character of theology waned. This was epitomized in Rudolph Bultmann. His intent was to move beyond objective truths and take subjectivity seriously. He drew upon Heidegger, for whom existence was essentially historical, but in Bultmann this became apolitical and individualistically focused. He is challenged by political theologians such as Johannes Metz and Dorothee Soelle who insist that persons cannot be understood apart from their social context. The current situation must be as critically analyzed as the past texts. Neither we nor Jesus can be wrenched from history.

We become aware of our dependency on society as well as being independent from its determinations. Unless this is part of our critical awareness, ideology is free to reign, and with it the perpetuation of an idolatrous situation. In this sense ideological critique becomes a logical and necessary extension of Bultmann's demythologizing project. Soelle asks, "Is it any less mythological to imagine that war, hunger and conditions that intensify our world's neuroses are simply determined by fate?"[10] Social as well as cosmological mythologies need to be challenged. We cannot consider the conditions that shape life as a fateful web from which faith magically redeems us. Faith does not lift us out of the world. Freedom is realized in everyday life, not removed from it.

Deprivatization is the term used to describe the theological task as both Soelle and Metz see it. This does not mean to make something less personal, but is, instead, an attempt to overcome depersonalization. The irony is that in defensively trying to protect or save what is one's own, in succumbing to the tendency to make things private, a person loses one's humanity, one's soul, one's connectedness with others. To understand persons as intrinsically social, and necessarily involved in social relations, means that the personal is political. Being a person involves a concrete social-political reality. One is shaped by and can in turn shape that reality. To do so is to be engaged politically. This implies a far broader understanding of politics. "Politics" becomes the arena of community production in which we collectively reclaim our human essence or freedom.[11]

In this situation, the designations "political" and "liberation" become almost synonymous, implying a similar if not identical theological perspective. Political theology is a helpful means for understanding European or North American workers' captivity to the historical structures of domination. It becomes linked with a stance of solidarity with those who are the poor, powerless, suffering victims of history—the focus of liberation theology. The link between political theology and liberation theology cuts through the underlying premise of class in American society, which is the need to set oneself apart from those who are the losers. It therefore begins to suggest what the redemptive dynamic will entail. Love lived in solidarity with victims, which is an expression of praxis, is at the heart of the theological project.

This identification with the victims, in contrast to modern theology's focus on the victors, provides the basis for critical realism to counter either superficial optimism (what reason can accomplish) or false pessimism (nothing can be done). What becomes irrational is not faith but so-called rational efforts to understand faith and reality. A critical perspective is needed to break through this rationality and emancipate human subjects. Critique attempts to break up the identity between reason and reality, which has the illusion of objectivity, and to uncover historical agency again, through the experience of the victims.

The critical dimension is an attempt to guard against sacralism, which tries to guarantee salvation for lip service to orthodoxy and obedience toward the powerful, dominant victors in history. In sacralism, "god" is identified with the victors. Sacralist religiosity distorts human life and represses moral freedom. [12]

Jesus' life-praxis broke with the ideological domination of sacralism and transformed sacralist values. Divine power became identified with victims not with domination and oppression. The consequence is a new faith and ideology, and a new relation of theory and praxis. Praxis continually seeks to make true that which faith knows—God identifies with victims. The problem is that the temptation of sacralism and domination emerges whenever God's presence or reign is identified with history. The challenge is to maintain a tension or nonidentity between God and history without lapsing into a dualism or paradox.

Not a New Dogmatic Theology

These perspectives of political theology suggest a theological project that will be quite different from dogmatic theology. This theology will be by the people in community with one another, as they discern what is happening in their social reality and discover what God is saying in the midst of it. Prime examples of this are the base communities of poor Latin American peasants. The people's theological work is developing and articulating the faith by which they can live. The pastor (or theological specialist) does not own, control, or determine either the people's struggles or their theological expressions. Instead, the pastor is a fellow worker in the theological task, who makes available to the people the textual resources and in-depth perspectives of the tradition.[13]

The fears of dogmatic theologians, who see such praxis-based theology leading to the *Aufhebung* of theology as they define it, are not totally without warrant.[14] Any attempts to sacralize certain formulations of the Christian faith and to impose them in the same way upon all are seriously questioned. This is because of the way redemption, the human subject, and history/society are conceived of by political theologians, and because the inherent critique resists all attempts at sacralism. Theology is always incarnated in historical mediations, which are susceptible to being made absolute and to being manipulated by sin. When that occurs, theological dogmas become idols, not symbols.

Theology must be wary of making certain articulations of the faith absolute. It must insist that God's Word brings judgment on all historical mediations, which must not be seen as absolute, but be open to new situations, different life experiences, and new discernments so the liberating possibilities of God's grace may be glimpsed anew.

By encouraging an ahistorical resignation and privatization of the faith, an ahistorical dogmatic theology may reflect the very problem that holds working-class and other victims of history in bondage. In this situation the redemptive, salvation dynamic of a gospel that transforms human lives enmeshed in social, economic, and political bondage is impeded. Political theologians view this state of resignation as the real problem of unfaith or atheism today. In this sense, such dogmatic theology may fall prey to the problem it claims to counter.

In the case of Lutheran dogmatic theology, salvation by God rather than historical emancipation by humans is presumed to be the focus. But that may be jeopardized by the way in which such a theology seeks to articulate and enforce certain interpretations of this divine activity—overlooking that any theology is at least in part a human project. These human attempts to defend God's saving grace may result in just the opposite, if they involve establishing certain formulations as absolute regardless of their historical impact. Ironically, the charge that some theologians might make against liberal, anthropocentric theologies, that they are too optimistic, or that they do not take the reality of sin seriously enough, are charges that may come back to haunt them instead.

In the next chapter we will suggest that the historical radicality of sin is to be taken more seriously from a political theological perspective—in a way that is faithful to the tradition that such dogmatic theologians seek to defend.

5

The Domination of Sin

Social, Historical Understandings of Sin

We are not engaged in developing new dogmatic, universal formulations of the Christian faith, but in reflecting on the social and personal reality of today's working people in light of the faith. This task requires a social-historical hermeneutic—a means of interpreting our contemporary social situation—that grows out of the perspectives discussed in the previous chapter.

How does grace or the gospel make a difference in relation to workers' reality in the world? This is the central pastoral issue. It is no small challenge, since "grace" has been identified as the notion most foreign to the theme prevalent in workers' reality, namely that "You are what you make of yourself." To address such a challenge, we must identify the way in which sin entraps persons in their sociohistorical situation.

In the case of American workers, it is unhelpful to begin by viewing sin as the activity of free subjects. The freedom that workers assume they have is contradicted by the reality of their unfreedom. In chapter 1 we observed that (1) working persons have lost a sense of themselves as historical subjects, and (2) the individualistic action they can take tends to perpetuate the reigning ideology that keeps the structures of bondage in place. Their actions are likely to increase their bondage to such structures by perpetuating the illusion that sin is only significant in the private arena.

A working-class person is perceived as sinning if that person fails to do what is dictated as right for the person's role as a worker, a parent, or a citizen. Sin is epitomized in the prohibitions of the Ten Commandments. Sins are those various acts in which a person steps out of line, disobeys those in authority, or engages in personal acts of immorality.

If a theological perspective on sin is to transform or liberate workers' experience in this society, then sin should not first be viewed in terms of individual personal acts but as a power of domination over individual experience. If workers do not experience themselves as active subjects in the world, then the starting point for discussing the phenomenon of sin in their lives is not what they individually have done but what has been done to them. The reality of having been *sinned against* must be encountered before sin can be understood as a personal responsibility. Sin as a historical, objective state of bondage, ruling over and distorting human life, must be given renewed emphasis. The language of social, structural, or corporate sin as developed in liberation and political theologies is crucial for this purpose. Yet this understanding must be kept in dialectic with understanding sin as evoking personal responsibility. The interior, personal dimension of sin derives from its sociohistorical character.

Sin from this perspective is experienced as an ahistorical power reigning over persons, but sin itself is not ahistorical. People sin in history by acting against God and God's intentions for human life. Human beings have created the institutions and ideologies that reign over workers' lives. Breaking open that realization is key in challenging the structural domination that sin engenders.

That the effects of sin are manifested in social structures is not a new discovery. Sin has been viewed as the cause behind social disorders or injustices throughout history. This causal connection often has been made in a way that places the present disorder in an ontological framework that lessens the urgency of tackling a specific historical problem: "After all, we'll always have problems like this."

However, appreciating the historical nature of sin is a modern development. An unjust, sinful situation does not happen by chance. Human responsibility lies behind it. Sin is a social, historical fact that is evident in oppressive structures of domination. Sin is not the result of demonic or evil forces separate from human beings, but becomes demonic or evil in its consequences. It begins to rule over people as an objective power, as if it were removed from historical relationships. In this sense, sin seems to become ahistorical. Although it is grounded in history, its manifestations oppose the meaning of history as a humanizing process.

One manifestation of sin is the destruction and repression of popular culture. A person begins to think, talk, act, and dress like the person he or she aspires to become. Left behind are those cultural expressions and communities that have sustained one and provided a sense of identity. To be in a state of sin is to be ruled by an alien power—the power of upward mobility. For black persons this alien power is the standard of whiteness; for working persons, whatever their color, it is the upward mobility standard of the American dream.

Western theologians, especially since the time of Augustine, have generally begun with a personal understanding of sin. They move from there to a more corporate understanding of sin as the institutional effects of individual actions. Social sin becomes the cumulative effect of individual sin. Individuals created and generated the structural realities that are now experienced as sinful. That realization is an important part of the critical process. Yet theologically interpreting workers' reality by beginning with a focus on individual sin is not particularly helpful.

First, the self-perception of many current victims of economic forces is not that of Enlightenment-inspired subjects of history, free to exercise personal responsibility. Rather, they see themselves as objects controlled by fate or a higher stratum, that is, the people in charge who presumably are the free historical agents.

Second, the control and domination today's workers experience usually feels so amorphous and anonymous that it is difficult to perceive it as due to personal acts or the sins of those in power. The persons who most directly exercise power over the workers—the managers—are often viewed as caught in the same vicious cycle. The owners or individual capitalists and their decision making are so obscure to most workers that it is hard to hold them personally responsible, except when they violate basic codes of morality. It seems impossible to accuse them of being personally accountable for decisions that directly and adversely affect the common good and workers in particular (such as the decision to move to where labor is cheaper). The competitive business system, foreign competitors, modernization, or union wages are blamed instead.

We propose that sin be viewed in terms of sociohistorical reality, not merely as the ahistorical cause behind the historical manifestations of domination and oppression. In this and in other ways, our proposal differs from Reinhold Niebuhr's, whose neoorthodox theology of sin has greatly influenced this country. His description of sin as a deeply religious problem and his resounding challenge of liberal theology's notion of moral progress in the life of the individual and in history are important. However, his anthropology and thus his theology of sin and grace are not defined in terms that are fundamentally social-historical. His presumption that persons are free historical subjects is not how working persons and others living under domination experience reality. According to Niebuhr, sin's essence is found in the vertical relationship to God, in a way that is removed from all social, economic, or political relationships. He does not find sin in social reality but in human nature, specifically in the paradox of finitude and freedom. Sin occurs when individuals are unwilling to put up with the basic ambiguity intrinsic in their creaturely and spiritual being. The anxiety arising out of this ambiguity causes persons to use freedom to make the self independent or the center of its existence. Pride becomes the chief manifestation of sin. Freedom is that which leads to sin, rather than that which is enslaved by sin. The freedom given by God is ahistorical and transcends social reality, rather than realized and exercised in relation to that reality. Although Niebuhr paid much attention to sin's social consequences, his theology emphasized the ahistorical, private individual and discouraged self-assertion, in other words, it encouraged those qualities that reinforces the plight of today's working people.

The twofold understanding of sin as an objective reigning power and sin as the subjective reality of personal guilt and responsibility is prominent within Western theological tradition. Sin is an illness, attitude, or collective blindness as well as freely chosen deeds. The tension between these two dimensions is crucial.

The subjective, sin-as-acts pole prevails in recent times because it is more compatible with a modern view. Social sin is viewed as the result of individuals acting freely. Individuals are personally responsible and can act otherwise. Sin is not our fate, even though we cannot escape the possibility of sin. Thus, the greed of the individual capitalist can be tempered. We can do better or try harder, but we will always have sin.

At times this view of human nature is accompanied by the mistaken assumption that God created us that way. At first this position seems more hopeful, especially regarding the possibility of ethical action, but it is likely to end up in a state of ahistorical resignation.

On the other hand, to interpret sin as a reigning power that feels like fate is to see sin as a religious issue. The structure of bondage itself must be broken through. This requires more than reversing individual acts of wrongdoing. The possibility of making the situation better with personal acts seems futile or remote. It is difficult to pinpoint any one enemy. The internalized reign of sin permeates our existence, whether we are oppressor or oppressed. We cannot conceive of another way of being. Sin is incarnate in the logic of the system and manifested in its contradictions and crises. The epitome of sin is to go along passively with this state of domination and bondage.

Here the prognosis is more severe, the possibility of human effort making a difference is initially more pessimistic. However, in breaking through this bondage, a more radical empowerment of human beings as historical subjects and shapers of their world is possible. Rather than being told they are subjects in spite of their lived reality of domination, a materially grounded, historically incarnate theology proclaims to workers that they are subjects in the midst of these historical realities. Thus social praxis to transform these realities becomes intrinsic to what it means to be created as historical subjects.

Rehistoricizing Luther's Theology of Sin

Social-structural understandings of sin in liberation and political theologies have generally not drawn upon Lutheran theological understandings. However, our diagnosis of the problem suggests the need to do so. Within such an understanding, the radical problem of sin is accentuated, which often results in a pessimistic interpretation of historical possibilities. However, this is not the only way to read or develop the implications of this tradition.

It can be reinterpreted to reveal the dominated reality and restore the possibility of historical praxis. We are reminded that human freedom has constituted what is now experienced as absolute and inevitable (e.g., the givens of capitalist society). Exposing sin need not shift the focus away from human activity in history, but can make that action truly historical—expressive of humans acting as subjects rather than reacting as dominated objects.

Distinctive Pauline-Lutheran emphases need to be reappropriated from a social-structural perspective. These emphases deal with and confront the many-faceted totality of domination that envelops workers. In this society most of workers' efforts are spent on trying to create the illusion that they are not really dominated. Therefore a deeper, more subtle understanding of sin is necessary in order to break through the illusion that one is one's own person, that is, not owned or dominated by others. A view that relies on autonomous subjects assuming historical responsibility on their own (as epitomized in the American dream) is inadequate because the problem is deeper than individual resoluteness. The self is in a state of bondage, largely because of the compensations it receives from the system of domination.

For Luther, sin is not primarily a set of acts but a state of unbelief. We are turned away from God. It comes not *from* us but *to* us. It is not mine but it becomes mine in that I succumb to it. I act, I sin. Speculative questions as to its origin are foreign to faith, which experiences sin as a demonic power enslaving humanity both collectively and individually.

The effect of sin is what is important. As described in Luther's writings, sin is deceptive, contradictory, and unknowable. It does not frighten or bite, but flatters and delights. While it is active it is not felt. We proceed smugly to the deed after we have forsaken our faith, unaware of what has happened to us or what we are doing.

Through our unbelief we fall from the Word into a lie. Our ungodliness lies in our denial of sin. Instead of confessing sin, we underestimate sin's power and declare our good works to be our righteousness. Doing what we think of as good or righteous is our sin. This presumption of righteousness becomes a huge monster—the worst kind of sin. In trying to grasp at our salvation, to make it our own rather than something given to us, we try to deny our status as sinners, thereby demonstrating before God that we are sinners. The real sin in which we have been ensnared prevents us from doing or working any good thing.[1]

This sin is exposed through the law, which provides a perspective enabling us to come to an awareness of the sin that is operating. The law unmasks the reality of our lives. In its basic Hebrew sense, it is the revelation of God's intention for us. We try to do what it prescribes but we continually fail to measure up. Thus, what was originally God's good intent toward us is experienced negatively. The law judges us, making us conscious of our various sins—the compounded individual sins of not measuring up. These sins are not the real problem. Preoccupation with them as the religious issue in our lives diverts attention from the root sin, namely, idolatry. We become preoccupied with symptoms rather than with causes. The law pushes us to this deeper level by its *increasing level of accusation,* showing us the futility of our efforts, which lead us away from rather than toward God and salvation.

The law has the theological potential to expose the self-contradiction in which American working people are trapped: doing the best they can plunges them deeper into sin, that is, into the illusion that they can make it on their own. This illusion becomes incarnated in the historical structures that reign over them, that is, the interlocking institutions and ideologies of American capitalist society. The law serves as the crucial interrupter that questions and surfaces what is going on, and, in Luther's schema, impels human beings toward God. What we expect to justify or enable us to get ahead instead condemns us. The cycle of betrayal in which workers play by the rules of the system, do not measure up, try harder, feel like failures, and eventually despair is exposed.

As noted in earlier, within working-class reality there is a strong sense of the importance of abiding by rules or laws, of living by a restricted code that clearly differentiates right from wrong. This consciousness is linked with a sense of standing before a god who is experienced as a judge or accuser. God becomes another authority who rules over and keeps subordinates in line, reminding them of the many ways in which they have not measured up in either God's or society's sight. God's dictates become operationally equivalent to the dictates of American capitalist society. Both intensify workers' feelings of individual guilt when they fall short.

Sin is experienced as the guilt arising from the commission or omission of certain acts. For Luther, this moralistic interpretation of sin is not a true knowledge of God or of God's proper work. As long as sin is seen in this way, it keeps persons in bondage to the real force of sin as that power that masters and enslaves them. Living according to the rules is mistaken as religious. The sin-as-acts perspective perpetuates the historical domination and keeps the idolatry within it from being unmasked. In this way, such sins work against the real intent of sin and law in Luther's theology, deterring movement from a moralistic to a theological interpretation of sin.

Sin's sense of inevitability arises because there seems to be no alternative to the individual's situation. Sin does not permit the soul to flee back to God but forces it into a flight away from God. The individual cannot acknowledge his or her entrapped situation—cannot "confess sin"—but hates God, who appears to become demonic.

Sin, a creation of humanity, becomes a monster destroying its creators. This tyrant character of sin points to its deepest dimension: the self-contradiction of the fallen world in its self-destructive character.[2] Sin acquires a transcendent, suprapersonal character that cannot be overcome in human terms, yet the tyrant remains human sin. This points to the profundity of human entrapment, which for Luther only a transcendent Christ can conquer. Sin dominates objectively and subjectively, becoming a closed totality.

In acknowledging our entrapment in sin we begin to question the assumption that we are living, speaking, and acting in a good, pious, righteous way. We begin to name or acknowledge our bondage, rather than living under the illusion that we are autonomous or in charge. This is the beginning of a new awareness, confession, and conversion.

There is evidence that Luther defined his theological understandings in relation to the reigning historical power of domination of his day—the institution of the papacy. The papacy was the most powerful institution ruling people's lives, with closely intertwined religious, social, and political dimensions. Luther viewed its institutional power of domination as a theological issue that threatened salvation.[3] His theological critique of the papacy, which he raised out of a pastoral concern for the people's consciences, for the sake of their salvation, became the means by which he began to break through the church's system of domination. He critiqued the dominating power of this institution in one of his most pivotal works, the Galatians Lectures of 1535.

The papacy as a historical structure of domination had become a challenge to the heart of justification. The interlocking powers of domination that American working people live under today are similar in impact. In a similar way a "tyranny of conscience" issue of faith may be at stake today. This suggests the potential for the central principle of the Reformation—justification by grace through faith—to come to the fore in its radically old yet new sociopolitical light, that is, in a way that challenges the heart of such persons' bondage to the "I-as-an-individual-can-make-it" ideology and the idolatry it upholds. Sin radically understood is about idolatry. As we discussed in chapter 3, idolatry lies at the heart of the American dream in which working persons have placed their trust. In the Reformation tradition naming sin is central for understanding God and God's grace, which alone can release persons from works-righteousness and empower them for historically transformative praxis.

Luther's theology is often viewed as antithetical to liberation theological perspectives, but when this theology of sin is viewed in relation to historical structures of domination, interesting parallels as well as areas of divergence with liberation or political theology begin to emerge.

Liberation Perspectives on Sin

Whereas much of the traditional view of sin focuses on the individual's subjective culpability for his or her actions, liberation theologians focus on the social manifestations of sin, the objective structures that seem to transcend individual agency. The aim is not to absolve personal responsibility (although at times that may be the unintended effect), but to deepen the sense of social sin.

Social sin resides in a group or in institutional arrangements. It is not produced by deliberate free choice but out of blindness. Gregory Baum describes its four levels.[4] The injustices and dehumanizing trends built into the various institutions of our collective lives are the first level. There is alienation in the workplace, profits are placed above people, bigger is better, workers and farmers feel their future is bankrupt. Family life becomes violent, communities have little sense of a common good, and racism, sexism, and classism are played off against each other.

The second level of social sin includes the cultural and religious symbols that legitimate and reinforce unjust institutions. Privatized, ahistorical interpretations of the Christian faith enable the ideology of the American dream to continue to legitimate the status quo.

Third, social sin refers to the false consciousness created by institutions and ideologies through which people get involved in destructive action as if they were doing the right thing. The achievement orientation of the dominant culture and its individualistic, competitive spirit result in relations of domination and subordination that mask our essential social needs, and generate a false rather than a communal consciousness.

Fourth, the collective decisions generated by a false consciousness increase the injustices in society and intensify the power of dehumanizing trends. If a company is not making the highest possible profit, it decides to relocate. If workers' sense of worth is based on at least being better than welfare recipients, their neighborhoods will vigorously organize to keep out the poor. The conscious, unjust decisions that those in power and authority make still constitute personal sin. "But the structures which such a corporate decision produces, and which in turn, by a logic of their own, inflict alienation on people, are bearers of social sin."[5]

Some biblical exegetes have explored this more social understanding of sin. According to José Miranda's exegesis of Romans 3, Paul's concern is not with individual salvation as we think of it but with the justice that society has long been awaiting. Justification and justice are more closely intertwined than is usually assumed in our society. "Individualism of salvation is the very negation of the faith of Jesus Christ."[6] Although sin enters the world through persons, it becomes incarnated in social structures. It is structured into civilization and the ideologies that support it. Sin's power increases even when people believe that they are conscientiously struggling against it.

Becoming aware of the oppression and naming it "sin" is a first but insufficient step. Liberation theologians, whose commitment is to the oppressed, usually do not devote much attention to the personal dimension of sin. Are persons absolved from personal responsibility because of the structural sin under which they live? What is the personal responsibility of those whose lives are determined by systemic domination? Personal responsibility emerges when people engage in the struggle against domination together. But how does that begin to occur in a way that accounts for the subjective reality of working people?

At this point Dorothee Soelle's discussions of sin are relevant. Sin, which is a disturbed relationship between human beings and God, disturbs and destroys our relation to ourselves, others, creation, and humanity. This parallels the fourfold manifestation of alienation (see chapter 2). Sin becomes synonymous with a kind of death in which we are cut off from life, but without even missing it or being conscious of its absence. It generates a sense of objective cynicism; we feel powerless. This begins to seem like a normal condition. We feel like victims of circumstance, with a passive attitude toward what is happening to us. Sin is "when life freezes over."[7]

Consequently, at the heart of this understanding of sin is the issue of idolatry, which is a kind of death. Capital becomes the god ruling over us; all else is subordinated to profit. Capital or making a profit is not in itself sinful or idolatrous, but does become an absolute for which human lives and communities are sacrificed.

Sin's sense of inevitability or social compulsion must be kept in close relation with personal responsibility or freedom. We are caught in the structural sin that has been given to us, but we sin personally by collaborating or going along with the domination and injustice that it embodies. Throughout the history of this doctrine, it has been difficult to keep this relation from collapsing on one side or the other, resulting in either a dismal pessimism or a naive optimism. When sin is experienced as a sense of powerlessness, its crucial connection with freedom is lost. Freedom must be reconstituted in a sociopolitical and not merely a privatized sense.

Such sin cannot be opposed by moral virtue, but by faith that a different kind of life is possible. The warrant for that is eschatological. Faith is the struggle against objective cynicism.[8] Breaking through the sense of fate or inevitability to a sense of personal responsibility occurs as people begin to see through this false world. This vision is enabled by God's grace and the promise of an open future that God unfolds. Such grace is discerned through our interaction with others, whereby we recognize the discrepancy between what is (the alienation and injustice) and the social-communal life (the shalom) that God intends for us.

The freedom that is unleashed is not the power to pursue one's goals without the interference of others, but the capacity of persons to recreate their world. It is the freedom to live out the communal "we-consciousness" that has been more resilient among working-class persons who have been less impacted by liberalism. It is the freedom to work with others, creating structures of mutuality rather than domination. When we do not exercise such freedom or moral responsibility we continue to exist in a sinful, dehumanizing condition.

Sin in Working-Class Reality

The pastoral implications for addressing sin in relation to the reality experienced by working persons begins to emerge. If we are sensitive to the sociohistorical context of working persons, we will understand how they might interpret the teachings and practices of the church.

The confession of sin is a regular part of most congregations' liturgy. Regardless of the words used, for most parishioners the ritual of confession evokes self-examination: What have *I* done wrong? That question is omnipresent in a society whose ideology continually engenders self-blame. What many workers are likely to hear behind that question is not only How have I wronged God? but How have I failed to measure up to the codes, ideology, and god of the American dream? Sin becomes operationally equivalent to class values. The notion of the church as a moral watchdog is deeply ingrained in many working people's upbringing.

More emphasis needs to be given to the question: How have we been wronged? If we are in bondage, how do we feel in bondage? In a society whose mythology is that the free individual can conquer all, these are not easy questions. The indignity of being wronged or enslaved is painful to acknowledge.

If sin is experienced first as a power of domination, then forgiveness of sins will not suffice as an all-purpose solution. To know that one's oppressor is forgiven does not relieve one's sense of being sinned against. Similarly, to receive forgiveness for one's sins of passivity does not necessarily activate a person. Those who have been dominated and oppressed need to be liberated and empowered, not merely placated.

Evoking a consciousness of the sociohistorical bondage of sin is likely to involve a long process of consciousness-raising. Increasing awareness of the pervasiveness of domination and the interlocking structures and ideologies of class is likely to evoke anger. Anger is directed at authority figures, for example, pastors who challenge rather than legitimate a fixed social order. Anger is directed at those structures that are beyond an individual's control, but that define workers' lives and seem to prevent them from being in charge of their own lives. Anger is also directed at the self for having been deceived and for not recognizing that these structures need not be absolutes. Anger is "a sign of resistance in ourselves to the moral quality of the social relations in which we are immersed."[9]

It is difficult to face the concurrent feelings of hopelessness and the need to take responsibility without a supportive communal context. The communal context within which such pain and anger is expressed mediates the experience of grace, empowering not only personal but societal transformation. God comes to be known through community as the one who sustains the self-in-community and reveals a future that is no longer synonymous with the American dream.

Faith and awareness of our relatedness to God emerge in the midst of sociohistorical reality, rather than as a transcendent dimension posited prior to and apart from that reality. The real issue of faith (versus works-righteousness) emerges in the midst of the real world where we live. Consequently, the distinction that Niebuhr and others make between the religious, vertical dimension of sin as rebellion against God and the moral, social, horizontal dimensions of sin as injustice becomes inadequate. All of it is rebellion against God.

The sociohistorical structures of domination become gods ruling over people's lives. The historical domination that working persons and others experience becomes both a religious and moral issue. Niebuhr's distinction may make sense for the powerful, but for the victims, the religious meaning of sin may be separated from the sociohistorical dimensions of life at the price of perpetuating the real sin or idolatry.

6

The Redemption of
American Working-Class Reality

Revisioning Redemption

Throughout our interpretation of working-class reality a yearning for salvation has been a persistent refrain. As the hope for realizing salvation through the promise of the American dream is betrayed, the intensity of that yearning increases. What is an appropriate theological response to this yearning? What speaks to the heart of sin in working people's reality and functions in a liberating rather than ideological way? How can we understand and communicate the reality of God's redemption amid the realities facing working-class people? This chapter will suggest directions for responses to these challenges, while recognizing that the actual responses are fleshed out in the midst of pastoral praxis.

The previous chapters have tried to expose the working-class dilemma that needs redemption. The domination workers experience within and outside of the workplace is so pervasive that it seems inevitable. Attempts made to escape from the reign of that domination are individualistic or ahistorical. They may seem to provide an escape hatch but actually fail to address the underlying structural situation.

The individual yearns for redemption from the situation rather than transformation or redemption of it. A dualism between the spiritual and the social-economic-political dimensions of life is perpetuated. It is hoped that social transformation—faith active in justice—will be a consequence of personal redemption. But if that redemption jettisons the individual away from the historical situation of domination, changing that situation becomes less urgent. Why worry about the domination if one is saved from or lifted out of that reality?

Salvation is necessarily social and historical. It is realized in the midst of a given historical reality. The spiritual and historical dimensions of life cannot be split asunder. Spiritual does not imply ahistorical, but a sense of fullness that takes on and transforms historical reality.[1] Transcendence does not remove us from history but empowers us to become more deeply immersed in it.

A theology of redemption is needed that breaks through the domination in a way that empowers the historical praxis of working people—enabling them to become subjects rather than remain objects. And yet redemption is not something human beings can achieve by observing the rules of any system. It is wrought by God. God inaugurates a new reality. Through redemption, human beings become more fully human subjects with one another in history, seeking to live out the justice that is the divine reality.

For this to occur, the domination or sin under which such persons exist must be challenged, transformed, or overcome. This domination is so pervasive that it is unrealistic to expect that individuals who are products of that domination to overcome it by themselves. The individual actions they take to attempt to free themselves from domination actually enslave them more deeply. Help is needed from outside. The sin of the world—the power of domination—must be conquered in a decisive, convincing way.

Yet if the "conquering" occurs according to a paradigm of power that replicates the world's structures of domination, with an all-determining powerful god controlling passive, historically powerless individuals, will the situation needing redemption really be redeemed? If working persons remain historically powerless after the objective reality of sin-as-fate is attacked, will anything really have changed? On the other hand, if the personal responsibility in sin is addressed apart from a redemptive address of the objective reality, the reign of sin will continue, generating the illusion that redemption of individuals will suffice.

Redemption must have an objective and subjective efficacy. It must be simultaneously external and internal in its effect. The domination of sin needs to be overcome. But the manifestations of sin in the subjective reality of working persons—privatization, individualism, and victimization—must be overcome as part of the same soteriological project, because the latter enable sin to maintain its hegemony over workers' lives. These three dynamics seduce working persons into submitting to the domination that is sin. The power of sin must be overcome in such a way that working persons are empowered to become historical subjects. Redemption is decisive, but the mark of its decisiveness is in how it impels liberating praxis.

The Redemption Wrought by God Through Christ

It is God who breaks the bonds of the domination under which the working class lives. God inaugurates a new reality through Jesus' life, death, and resurrection. The historical Jesus, who was crucified on the cross by the powers of domination of his day and raised from the dead by God, is the source of salvation from the bondage. How can that become meaningful and also transform working people's plight?

Jesus' life and the message he preached are important in understanding the meaning of his death and resurrection. Only a God clothed in concrete events will suffice, that is, a God whose meaning became manifest through the liberating praxis in Jesus' life. Jesus engaged in a liberating praxis by standing with those oppressed by the dominating systems of his day—religious, political, economic, and gender-related. The Spirit of God was upon him to preach good news to the poor and to set free the oppressed (Luke 4:18). The poor, the sick, the social outcasts, and the women discerned something new in him. The systems that treated them with scorn as trivial objects were challenged through his actions and his proclamation of God's reign. He had a sovereign disregard for class, racial, and sexual differences that put some persons above others. Jesus rejected self-enclosed systems and the subservience they demanded. His liberating praxis was born out of a profound and intimate experience of a relational God who gives and receives, who empowers rather than dominates human beings.

The God revealed through Jesus is a God who refuses to associate with human attempts to dominate. Jesus called his followers not "servants," which connotes hierarchy, but "friends," which connotes mutuality (John 15:15). He was not a hero for anyone's system; rather, he initiated a transformation of the structures and operating assumptions of the world's systems, including the religious establishment.

Jesus' crucifixion was the consequence of such a life. It more fully revealed the character of God's entry into human history—not as a dominating victor but as a God who identifies with the human condition. The God revealed on the cross is the antithesis of the gods of class and the American dream, whose dogmas of progress and upward mobility veil the pain of people's dreams betrayed. The crucifixion represents the death of the threefold idol of individualism-victimization-privatization. Jesus died publicly and in solidarity with victimized humankind.

The cross proclaims a decisive end to the system of striving for self-sufficiency and its image of the self-made person. We are so bound to these illusions that God comes through what we least expect—suffering and death. God does not come to legitimize or rationalize suffering but to identify with us in the midst of it.

Through such solidarity of God-with-us, we are empowered to be more than passive victims who are dominated by fear. The presence of God opens up an expectancy that is sustained amid the pain. The resurrection of the crucified Jesus proclaims that amid helplessness and death, the God of freedom and justice-seeking love is revealed in radical distinction to any god who would subjugate or keep us dominated by fear.[2]

The resurrection qualifies the cross as an eschatological saving event in history. The resurrection reminds us of who suffered and died, namely, Jesus, who refused to live according to class mandates. He refused to engage in self-justifying schemas, refused to try to be god, thereby becoming the revelation of God. The resurrection proclaims that what occurred on the cross was "of God," that it was God's inauguration of a new way of life, a new reality, a new creation. Empirically it looked like defeat, but from the perspective of resurrection faith it was the victory of life over the death that is sin. The resurrection is the reign of God dawning in power, a power that is understood quite differently because of the life praxis of the historical Jesus and because of what happened on the cross. The resurrection's eschatological aspect makes it clear that God "condemned sin in the flesh" (Rom. 8:3), not to reward Jesus with individual power, but to provide his project of the kingdom with the power needed to turn it into reality.[3]

Fundamental changes in the whole social structure of reality are initiated. Rather than a notion of a God who needs to be satisfied through the payment of debt or sacrifice, the relationship between God and the world is changed. As Luther noted, if the basic structure is one of a debt needing to be paid, as in an economic or legal transaction, then nothing new breaks in. Instead, God gives Godself to us in such a way that we become God's.[4] We are adopted as God's children, and become part of a universal brother- and sisterhood with Christ.

As Paul makes clear, especially in his Letter to the Romans, God justifies us by faith. Faith becomes the antithesis of acting to save or justify ourselves. Faith permeates our whole being and acting, so that our actions become bold, creative, and gratuitous, destined for life rather than death. Faith, which enables us to forget our fears and sterile ways of accounting for what we have done, makes possible human work, that is, unalienated work that bears the stamp of human beings and defies death.[5] The creative love that arises out of faith fights against the mechanisms of domination and continues to hope against hope, empowered by the resurrection's eschatological promise. As Dorothee Soelle paraphrases Rom. 6:12-14:

> The system of injustice shall therefore no longer determine the way you live, so that you run after false dreams. . . . But give yourself to God, as those who having once been without ability to communicate

and without power have now come alive. . . . For the system of injustice will be unable to break you, since you are subject, not to the force of circumstances, but to grace.[6]

Living Faith *Coram Deo*

Because of Christ's life, death, and resurrection we are able to protest against domination. Faith is not separate from historical experience, but provides the perspective enabling that experience to be critiqued. It opens up the possibility of naming the contradiction between the American dream's promise and what working persons are actually experiencing (how the dream is being betrayed). We are reminded of our "power of origin" (Tillich) and empowered to engage in a praxis that counters the passive resignation of victimization.

God creates right relationship with us through justification by grace through faith. This *coram deo* (in the presence of God) relationship is lived out in our relationships with ourselves, others, and the whole created order. We are freed to engage in justice-making in the world. The *coram deo* relationship provides a way of perceiving all of reality as being in the presence of God. This is a theological perspective on reality, a way of knowing the world. This perspective threatens society's structures and ideologies because it challenges them on their own grounds, namely, their tendency to assert themselves as absolute and autonomous. Faith is the basis for this challenge, faith that is opposed not to the world but to the godlike quality the world acquires, that is, its sinfulness.

The person of faith finds her or himself in the midst of this conflict over what is true reality. Through *coram deo* we have a perspective on what is real—we are justified, redeemed, becoming new creations—yet we still live in the reign of sin, immersed in its conflicts and struggling against

93

its power and manifestations. We are not removed from the struggle with sin, but we have a new perspective through faith. Law, sin, and death continue to confront us, despite reassurances of eschatological victory. Conversion, as a turning from unfaith (autonomy) to faith (theonomy) is a continuing saga in the history of our lives.

The opposition is not between God and the world, but between God and the sin that becomes incarnate in the structures and ideologies of society. The opposition is between God and the death toward which the threefold reign of individualism, victimization, and privatization leads. The world enters into contradiction with itself whenever it becomes an unquestioned absolute, its own god. This self-contradiction is grasped *coram deo*. Through this lens of faith, the world becomes "mere" world again, not that which would rule over and dominate working persons' experience. The world is put into perspective, taken seriously as a human creation, and thus not its own ultimate. We are called to responsibility and enabled to challenge the world whenever it tries to become absolute. This is an issue of faith. If we allow the historical structures of domination to continue unabated, we are cooperating with and perpetuating sin. For Luther this involved a communal struggle against sin,[7] as it also must for working people today.

What then is overcome? An objective, victorious overcoming of the structures of domination is unlikely to be evident. That is an eschatological reality. Following Jesus involves living in defiance of the subjective power of domination, which begins to disempower its objective power. Christ unmasked the quasi-divine authority of these structures, which in and of themselves were not evil or contrary to God's creative will. When unmasked they lose their totalitarian, conserving hold on life—their unmasking is the beginning of their defeat.[8] The threatened insecurity, the sting of the powers and principalities, is overcome. The powers of domination no longer have an idolatrous hold over workers' lives. As objective realities they still reign, and need to be resisted and struggled against. But now we are empowered to do so together, as part of an ecclesial community of resistance. Realizing that the idolatry of the system that victimizes us has been broken through the resurrection becomes more real for us when we act in defiance of the system's absoluteness.

Redemption liberates historically created realities from becoming absolutes. It impels historical praxis, which is activity that counters domination. Included in this is a critique of a dominating "God" who is depicted in such a way as to rob us of our responsibility for enacting right relationship in history. It is not that working persons are controlled by a new, more beneficent power. This would compound rather than solve the basic problem of disempowerment. But *coram deo*, they are defined by another reality for the sake of transforming the situation that generates the contradictions or betrayed dreams that they experience. This other reality, or reign of God, is a saving reality that necessitates praxis. Its meaning emerges in doing. A fuller sense of who we are emerges as we are empowered to engage in praxis that by its very nature undercuts the domination.

The Praxis of Redemption

Social praxis is the complex of social, political, economic, and ideological activity that transforms sociohistorical relationships and our awareness of a given social reality. Through praxis we enter into an active, dynamic relationship with our external reality. We are not separate from it, but are changed in the process of trying to change it.

Praxis is more than the implementation or application of a previously defined theory. It is more than putting faith into practice, or making Christianity practical or relevant. It arises from within the experience of oppression and is set over and against the prevailing society and cultural consciousness. The transformative change that praxis seeks is both societal and individual because of how enmeshed society is in the individual. To change one is to change the other.

The primacy given to praxis by liberation and political theologians is often misunderstood. It is not that praxis takes away from the gracious activity of God, who establishes right relationship with us. It does not pass over what has been actualized in Jesus Christ, but enables that historical event to be more deeply understood in the midst of our historical situation. The praxis arising out of our understanding affects our interpretation of the Jesus event. That interpretation becomes the basis for a new praxis. Praxis is a mediating factor in communicating the mystery revealed in Jesus Christ.

Getting involved in the lives and issues of people opens up new theological understandings. As the congregations I pastored began to reach out and get involved in the needs of people, and in the correlative issues of social injustice, central understandings of the Christian faith became far more meaningful in the lives of some of the members. Praxis became the mediation of a deepened faith.

The struggles involved in sharing the church building and occasional celebrations with a Black Holiness congregation opened up new theological understandings of who our brothers and sisters in Christ really are. Reaching out to severely disabled young adults in a nearby facility caused us to hear and see the gospel in new ways through their handicaps and suffering. We joined them in confronting the city council over the justice issue of a stoplight—an activity that brought us together as an empowered community of faith. Parishioners who finally began to speak up about the demeaning control they experienced in the workplace, and who shared the memory of their own working-class histories of suffering, suddenly discovered a touchstone with the suffering peasants of El Salvador, whose tragic plight faintly resembled their own struggles.

None of these examples resulted in dramatic visible changes in the praxis of these working-class parishioners, but each served as an important pivot in how they perceived their world and their relation to it. Each was the beginning of a radical conversion in which outsiders became signs of what God is about. In each case, groups that we and our upwardly mobile cultural values and practices generally overlooked or looked down upon, became channels for the inbreaking of God's grace. Through these relationships redemption became more evident in our common sociohistorical reality. As these signs of grace and redemption became manifest, some members preferred to cling to the still reigning power of sin and its alienating worldview of dominated and dominating— reluctant to accept that black, handicapped, and poor people might be means of God's grace.

In proposing that social praxis be seen as mediating redemption, we are not suggesting that this praxis is necessarily highly evident in public terms. It is difficult for praxis to be determined or judged from the outside. But the marks of transforming social praxis seem to be at least threefold.

1. Praxis resists or counters domination, and links us with others in our situation rather than further alienating us from them. From out of that relationship or solidarity, working-class cultural expressions begin to emerge. These help to counter privatization, ahistoricity, and passive victimization. A workers' culture—songs, code words, and expressions of scorn for the higher-ups—provides the beginning by proclaiming, "Hey, we're somebody!" in the face of forces that would deny this.

2. Social praxis arises out of some sense of the domination people live under, which needs to be viewed critically rather than cynically accepted as inevitable. For example, what happens to workers here is intertwined with what happens to workers in Asia. In this country, what happens to workers in the city is not unrelated to what happens to farmers in the country. Thus, whatever we do is not done in a privatized, ahistorical sense but with at least minimal awareness of both its limits and possibilities for wider transformative impact.

3. Praxis is shaped from below rather than from above. It is in intentional solidarity with the victims rather than victors of society. Those who are the least become our reference point, rather than those on a vector of upward mobility. Thus, unexpected coalition-building becomes possible for the sake of common interests that previously were viewed as antagonistic. The power of the crucified and resurrected one enables us to break through the us-versus-them bondage and form a new "we."

The Memory of
Working-Class Suffering

The contradiction between the promise of the American dream and the reality of working people's lives must be exposed. The victimization that workers experience when the dream is betrayed must be expressed and given a historical context if there is to be a transition from passive resignation to active transformation of their situation. This occurs by means of the process that Metz calls "the memory of the history of suffering."[9]

Muting the memory of suffering is pervasive in our society, and especially among working-class people. The ideal life is free from suffering. Apathy increases when the assimilation of middle-class notions of what to strive for replaces concern for others.

> This doesn't mean that apathetic people in the industrial nations don't suffer—let alone that they are happy. What they lack is an awareness of their own suffering and a sensitivity for the suffering of others. They experience suffering, but they "put up with it," it doesn't move them. They have no language or gestures with which to battle suffering.[10]

The pleasant, nostalgic aspects are remembered, but the negative memories of alienation, struggle, and failure are forgotten or repressed. These memories are too painful. People identify themselves according to upwardly mobile values, according to what they or their children hope to become, rather than in terms of whom they have left behind.

The communication of suffering is crucial if dominated people are to move from passive, apathetic endurance toward liberation. As this occurs, we find ourselves in the presence of God. If people cannot speak their pain they will be destroyed by it, swallowed by apathy—dead! Communicating suffering is the beginning of a faith-motivated praxis, of transformation, of life, and of theology. "The mute God presupposes people who have been rendered mute."[11]

Breaking through the silent and silencing illusion of no suffering is the beginning of a movement from death to faith. Persons move from a mute, powerless resignation in which domination feels so total as to preclude any questioning to a stage where they can begin to communicate what it is like. The suffering begins to be articulated: the fear of losing one's job by stepping out of line, the psychological monotony, the physical toll on one's body and health, the sense of failure in never quite making it. As a young gravedigger articulated it,

I make good money, I've got some seniority, my bills are paid, and my car is running. Hey, not bad, eh?! Then some ridiculous office systems commercial comes on and we're all reminded that we don't have offices, secretaries, car phones or bad toupees and it's back to moping in our shots and beers again.[12]

Negative memories are crucial for correlating theology and sociopolitical life. Remembered suffering serves a subversive and thus a practical function. We are reminded of the history of the defeated, of our history as a dominated people. Meaning is not reserved for the conquerors or the affluent middle class. Memory shocks us out of resigning ourselves or accepting our present situation as fate. By remembering and naming the suffering we begin to take away power from the cause of the suffering, be it the system, the boss, mass culture, or a dominating god. Memory mobilizes a dangerous tradition, which becomes a liberating force for resisting domination.

The possibility of solidarity with other victims emerges. Other oppressed coworkers, either here or in other parts of the world, begin to become a part of who I am—they become present—as I move from an individualistic to a more corporate understanding of the self. As long as my identity is wrapped up in making it, I am threatened by the commonalities between myself and others who are victims.

Our memory is of the history of suffering. We remember those who are victims of social amnesia because they did not make it. They remained working class, either passively accepting their imposed plight or they became hard livers who rebelled against it. We remember and analyze the history of workers' struggles in this country and around the world, and raise up some working-class saints. We remember the current victims of plant shutdowns or the farm economy, and others for whom the promise of high-tech jobs is a cruel illusion. We look at structural causes of workers' expressions of suffering and recognize these as not inevitable, but as human-caused and thus transformable. We anticipate the future as the future of the oppressed, made possible because of the empowering memory of Jesus the crucified, whose suffering and resurrection hold open the future for all other victims. God-in-Christ does this in order to safeguard human praxis, not at its expense.

The Christian tradition keeps alive the memory of the crucified Christ as a dangerous memory of freedom in the social systems that control persons. The memory of Jesus compels us not to give up but to recommit ourselves to a social praxis that changes ourselves and our social situation in light of a future guaranteed by God. The eschatological dynamic of change that Christ embodies is lodged in the midst of that which dominates and dehumanizes working persons. Reflecting upon concrete suffering in light of the cross and resurrection gives us a glimpse of a new human way of life. Salvation history becomes secular history in which meaning is imparted to forgotten or suppressed hopes and sufferings.

A Spirituality of Social Empowerment

If workers' dilemma is characterized by the lack of a sense of themselves as active subjects in the world, if they are thus dominated and alienated from the divine intent, then that situation needs to be exposed and redeemed. If exposing the dilemma is intrinsic in the work of redemption, then redemption cannot be interpreted in a way that reinforces this lack of historical praxis. Instead, a spirituality of empowerment unfolds.

First, working persons become more aware of the contradictions and betrayals in which they are enmeshed: although they work hard, they do not achieve the promised goal; they

101

are told that they matter, but their experience is that they do not; the ideologies to which they have pledged their faith and vote deliver for a few, but not for them. When these and other contradictions become apparent, such persons feel betrayed, they cry out. They move from apathy or passivity to a mood of protest.

Second, the sociohistorical structures and ideologies that generate these contradictions begin to be named as sin. The focus of the problem shifts from being a dilemma of not having measured up to a sense of the corporate entrapment in which one is caught up with others. Rather than this sense of social sin passing over personal responsibility, it points to the historical relationships that constitute what seems like an absolute, inevitable reigning power, and opens up the possibility for transformative praxis. Human subjects generated the domination; human subjects can counter the domination.

Third, for this to happen, a radical change or reorientation is required. This conversion is radical because of the deep, pervasive, and interlocking sociohistorical manifestations of sin. It occurs at that point when giving in to cynicism and hopelessness seems unavoidable—when our attempts to rescue ourselves have run out. At that point a supernatural rescuer is not likely to rush in. That did not happen for Jesus on the cross, nor does it for us. God acts to redeem the world, not to redeem us away from the world. Instead, the world where domination and alienation are experienced comes into view as a historical world constituted by human praxis. We discover what it means to stand *coram deo* rather than be determined by the world. Our powerlessness and hopelessness are transformed into active struggle. We no longer need to acquiesce to inevitable domination. We realize that we can choose Life.

The illusion that there will be no new sufferings is stripped away. This brings us to the fourth step in the

spirituality of empowerment. We move into a praxis of solidarity with others who have been and are victims. Victims
become subordinate, dependent, and "ineffective—unable
to effect good—until they are able to reclaim their power,
which they can do only in relation."[13]

Suddenly, the barriers that separate us from the more
public victims in our society and world begin to fall, along
with the us-versus-them identity essential in propping up a
sense of identity in this class society. We begin to orient
ourselves in *relation with* rather than over-and-against the
oppressed. Instead of salvation sought in what we make of
ourselves in relation to others, salvation emerges through
our solidarity with those who have not made it. No longer do
we need the needy for our own self-justification. We begin to
discover more deeply what grace and redemption are from
this perspective. We no longer need to cling to the promise of
the American dream and its related ideologies to save us.

Individualism, victimization, and privatization separate
us from God. The meaningful overcoming of this alienation
from God—redemption—occurs when individualism, victimization, and privatization are transformed. All three are characterized by a lack of social praxis. Their transformation
unleashes such praxis. Acts of individualism in trying to make
it are replaced with the praxis of persons-in-community,
who cannot be saved apart from each other. Salvation occurs
within a communal matrix. The transcendence or decisive
break with the way things are—the break with privatization
—plunges us into history and impels our praxis. The oppressed
know only too well the experience of being dominated objects,
and hence the absence of grace. Praxis that identifies with
their victimization, but at the same time is determined that
victimization not be the end of the story, is not praxis that
violates grace but is open to the possibility of grace making a
difference in how we live our lives in the world. The lock of

works-righteousness that determines our value in this society is broken open. Solidarity with the oppressed, who have nothing by which to commend themselves, mediates grace, because such solidarity reveals that redemption is not in what we make of ourselves.

To experience grace is to experience human historicity.[14] Grace or redemption acquires sociohistorical meaning, specifically through the memory of the history of suffering. Realms that have become closed or reified are challenged. There is a decisive break with the worldview of upward mobility that is focused on what one can make of oneself, and based on an individualism or self-sufficiency that is a rejection of grace. If this break does not occur, grace will remain an individualized, spiritualized concept that either reinforces or is seen as irrelevant to the works-righteousness endemic in American culture.

Grace is both gift and task. The grace of God becomes particularly evident when we choose to stand with the oppressed. In refusing to accept the givenness of those structures that victimize all of us, we become more open to the working of God's grace. Our acceptance of God's gracious gift engages us in the task of struggling against injustice in society.

Such social praxis is the opposite of works-righteousness. Faith shapes and informs praxis.[15] A commitment to solidarity with "the least" emerges out of faith, and in defiance of the pervasive works-righteousness rule that governs life and defines salvation in our class society. Only as we are defined according to something other than this hegemonous rule can we enter into such a praxis.

This chapter has outlined a theological process that provides the basis for a more effective and progressive political empowerment of America's working class. This political praxis is more communally based, more consciously related to structures, more intentionally in coalition with other victims, and thus more radical than the predominant options on the present political landscape. Surrounded as we are by counterrevolutionary, right-wing appeals to working people, the task could not be more urgent.

We see the church as the place where this process begins to occur, as it proclaims the embodiment of the gospel of redemption amid the realities of people's lives. The religious community can provide a place to stand, with a perspective different from the situation of domination. It can become a community of resistance, living out the hope of the reign of God, in solidarity with the oppressed. This may involve a considerable shift in how most ecclesial communities view themselves. We will conclude with some reflections on what such a shift might mean.

7

Church as Midwife
of New Communities of Justice

We have proposed an interpretation of God's redemption through Jesus Christ that involves the transformation of American class realities. Classism is opposed to God's gracious activity. How then can the church more faithfully witness to God's good news for all people, and particularly for American working people? How can local congregations' life and priorities be shaped differently? What are some implications for how evangelism, religious education, liturgy, pastoral care, social ministry, and stewardship are viewed and carried out?

First of all, the church can become far more intentional in countering classism in its internal life. Classism is reflected in the ways values and priorities of those of a higher class are unconsciously imposed upon those of a lower class. The way we as a church do things, which reflects our class position, is identified with what it means to be Christian. The so-called successful church is the upwardly mobile church, as reflected in its material acquisitions as well as in its activities. New congregations are usually "planted" in areas where they can be expected to become self-sufficient in a short time. One joins a church of one's own class or that reflects one's upwardly mobile aspirations.

Institutional churches are captives of classism. Challenging this is extraordinarily difficult because people's voluntary church affiliation is strongly influenced by society's assumptions. To challenge these assumptions is to risk losing members. The point at which persons may possibly be open to a challenge of this captivity is when they are experiencing the outright betrayal of the assumptions embedded in the American dream. The pastoral task is not to assure congregation members that they will soon be back on track. Rather, the experience of betrayal must, on theological grounds, be opened up to critical questions. Who is God and how is God active in this situation? The pastoral, pedagogical, and evangelistic tasks flow together at this point. The pastoral necessitates prophetic questioning, religious education evokes critical social consciousness, and evangelism occurs in relation to a given social context.

What is crucial is the realization that one does not stand alone, but that God sets us within a community of faith. As in the early church at Pentecost, we together are empowered by God's Spirit to resist the idolatrous hold of society's assumptions. The community of faith is called to be faithful to God rather than to the idol of the American dream. It is called to become an ecclesial community of resistance to the powers of domination that reign over people's lives. It is called to resist death and witness to life.

The church can be key in countering the trinity of individualism-victimization-privatization. This involves reenvisioning some of the church's central liturgical, diaconal, and stewardship activities.

1. As a counter to individualism, the church is a place where *communal memory and activity* come alive. Its liturgical life is one of re-membering—of putting us back together in relation to God and in relation to one another. It is a place where painful as well as joyous memories can be celebrated.

The church's liturgical life is communal experience par excellence, where we discover and celebrate what it means to be a *people* rather than only isolated individuals. At its best, the church becomes a "free space"[1] from the powers of domination that structure our lives in the world. Within this space, people can rework and reappropriate ideas and themes from the biblical tradition in ways that bring forth hidden, potentially subversive meanings. Communal associations can and do occur in the church that cut across the boundaries and dictates of class. Millionaires and paupers may find themselves kneeling together at the altar rail. How can what is nurtured there make a difference beyond that space?

Such free space, and the communal associations that develop there, serve not only as a humanizing buffer or retreat from the world, but can be a means for empowering collective action in pursuit of a common good. Through the revitalization of memory and communal ties, it can become a breeding ground for democratic change. Elements of the tradition (e.g., we are created in God's image to become historical subjects) become resources for participating in democratic activity that crosses bounds of race, ethnicity, gender, and class.

2. In this sense, the church can be an effective counter to the victimization that many experience in society. We are not passive victims of whatever is happening to us. God empowers us to be *active, historical subjects* in the world.

It is through the structures of community life, which sustain and reproduce a group's shared bonds of historical memory and culture, that an oppressed people begin to come to self-consciousness. Through their activity in new contexts, groups may acquire public skills, reinforce democratic values, and form new links between subcommunities into larger networks and organizations. And it is through such processes that a powerless people constitutes itself as a force for democratic transformation of the broader social structure and as a school for its own education in a democratic sensibility.[2]

Some of the more promising examples of such empowerment are found in congregation-based community organizations.[3] Much of this organizing builds upon insights set forth by Saul Alinsky a half-century ago, but often with significant variations from his confrontational style. The basic purpose of community organizing is to unify and empower people in a community, so they can begin to change their situation, and in turn be changed (i.e., empowered) through their involvement.

Organizing is done around people's values or self-interests. Rather than an individual or family facing a problem in isolation from others, their problem or issue becomes linked with that of others, including those of a different race or class position. For example, addressing a garbage pick-up problem in a community is likely to be in the self-interest of blacks and whites, rich and poor. Organizing around such an issue helps build the organization, enabling it to address more substantial issues later.

Relationship building, which is what community involves, can become an end in itself, not merely a means to an end. Community organizing builds upon the democratic tradition by going beyond electoral politics and emphasizing public discussion and negotiation aimed at holding business and government accountable to the common good. Community economic development is increasingly the focus of such organizing efforts. The emphasis is on systemic change, rather than on the organization providing direct service to address a problem. For example, the focus is not on opening food pantries to help those who are unemployed after a factory closes, but on how to keep the plant from closing down without accountability to the community it leaves behind.

This is a significant departure from the church's usual approach to social ministry, which has been based on finding and helping those who are victims. Social ministry has frequently connoted helping or offering services to the needy in a way that tends to perpetuate patterns of paternalism and dependency. Those who engage in such initiatives typically do so because it makes them feel good. "There but for the grace of God go I" is often piously uttered as the motivation for helping those less fortunate, even though such persons sense that individual effort rather than God's grace may be the determinative factor. Social ministry in this sense helps to keep class relationships in place. In contrast, community organizing transforms persons from being dependent victims into subjects who are empowered to change their situation. Community organizing tends to affect the entire congregation, whereas social ministry typically is the domain of a small number of members of a special committee.

3. As the church begins to address *public issues* more effectively, it provides a counter to privatization. What used to be seen as private pains become public issues. Rather than carrying home most of the pain of what it means to be workers, expecting solace and nurture within this private refuge, the focus shifts to those systemic factors generating or contributing to the pain. The links between family, work, and community become more evident. The church becomes a more effective public actor, not necessarily through its official social statements or encyclicals, but by being "of the people." Pastoral immersion in the struggle of the people pulls the church into prophetic critique of the structures and priorities that generate the pain.

This brings us to a central yet often neglected responsibility of the church's stewardship: to work so that structures and institutions more fully reflect God's intentions for human life in community. As a community of resistance, the church must be bold in interrupting the powers of domination, in challenging the practices and priorities that destroy persons and communities. Then it can work together with those who have the expertise for creating more just policies and structures. The church may not have ready-made answers, but it can provide the space, support, and vision that enable the tough questions to be asked and the difficult search for new options to begin. Ideally, it can be a place where working persons and corporate executives meet and listen to one another—together deliberating over key public issues.

Perhaps the reason that communities of faith find it so difficult to struggle together is that typically we have given short shrift to the work of the Holy Spirit, the mysterious third person of the Trinity who has the task of attending to relationships. Because we as a male-dominant society are so enthralled with the myth of the self-contained, self-possessed, autonomous individual who has all the answers, such an image has also been projected onto God. Bonding with others, which is what the church is called to do, is seen as a sign of dependence, need, and weakness.

Yet the presence of God becomes most powerful in our lives and history, not as a God who controls us and provides the answers for us, but a God who empowers us to work together on the answers. We tend to adjust or compromise our faith to correspond with what is, rather than discover the strength embedded in the alternative ethic activated by the Spirit.

We need to take seriously the Spirit's power to challenge unjust structures or relations in the world, and to move us toward a worldview different from the one common in this class society. Rather than competitive relationships that set us over and against one another, the Spirit invites us into a new community in which we are co-subjects with one another, cooperating and cocreating just relations. The church as a community is called to work together with other communities, ever vigilant in challenging those ways through which classism is perpetuated and ever diligent in witnessing to the Reign of God—a vision of just relations, which is at the core of our Christian hope. It is this hope that enables the church to participate as a midwife in the emergence of new communities that are participatory and empowering of all.

Notes

1. Introduction

1. Richard Sennett and Jonathan Cobb, *The Hidden Injuries of Class* (New York: Knopf, 1972), 241.

2. Stephen J. Rose, *The American Profile Poster* (New York: Pantheon Books, 1986), 9.

3. Based on a comparison of statistical tables of "non-agricultural workers on payrolls" from *Monthly Labor Review*, U.S. Department of Labor, Bureau of Labor Statistics, vol. 103: 12 and vol. 112: 12.

4. Jean Mayer and J. Larry Brown, "More Prosperity, More Hunger," *New York Times*, Saturday, February 25, 1989, op. ed. page.

5. W. N. Grubb and R. H. Wilson, "Sources of Increasing Inequality in Wages and Salaries, 1960–1980," *Monthly Labor Review* 112 (April 1989): 4, 11.

2. The Dilemma of Working People

1. Arthur Marwick, *Class: Images and Reality in Britain, France and the USA Since 1930* (New York: Oxford University Press, 1980), 112.

2. See, among others, Harry Braverman, *Labor and Monopoly Capital* (New York: Monthly Review Press, 1974), 293ff.

3. Ibid., 325, 371.

4. *Monthly Labor Review* 111 (December 1988): 12.

5. Rose, *The American Profile Poster*, 13.

6. John C. Raines and Donna Day-Lower, *Modern Work and Human Meaning* (Philadelphia: Westminster Press, 1986), 53, 76.

7. Michael Lewis, *The Culture of Inequality* (Amherst, Mass.: University of Massachusetts Press, 1978).

8. Joseph T. Howell, *Hard Living on Clay Street* (Garden City, N.Y.: Doubleday Anchor Books, 1973).

9. Raines and Day-Lower, *Modern Work*, 53.

10. Lillian Breslow Rubin, *Worlds of Pain: Life in the Working-Class Family* (New York: Basic Books, 1976), 135.

11. "No Joke: Possible Hazards from VDTs Radiate Concern," *Chicago Tribune*, 21 July 1986, sec. 4, p. 14.

12. Barbara and John Ehrenreich, "The Professional-Managerial Class," in Pat Walker, ed., *Between Labor and Capital* (Boston: South End Press, 1972), 19.

13. The categories and analyses of workplace control are from Richard Edward, *Contested Terrain: The Transformation of the Workplace in the Twentieth Century* (New York: Basic Books, 1979).

14. The relation between women's continued poverty and the growth of the service sector is discussed in Joan Smith, "The Paradox of Women's Poverty . . . ," in Barbara C. Gelpi et al., eds., *Women and Poverty* (Chicago: University of Chicago, 1986), 121–40.

15. Michael B. Katz, *The Underserving Poor* (New York: Pantheon Books, 1989), 69.

16. Edward, *Contested Terrain*, 192.

17. Roderick Martin and R. H. Fryer, "The Deferential Worker?," in Martin Bulmer, ed., *Working-Class Images of Society* (London: Routledge & Kegan Paul, 1975).

18. Andy Banks and Jack Metzger, "Participating in Management," *Labor Research Review* 14 (Chicago: Midwest Center for Labor Research, 1989), 53.

19. Michael Lerner, *Surplus Powerlessness* (Oakland, Calif.: Institute for Labor and Mental Health), 24.

20. Ibid., 84.

21. Barbara Garson, *All the Livelong Day* (New York: Penguin Books, 1977), 221.

22. Bertell Ollman, *Alienation: Marx's Conception of Man in Capitalist Society* (Cambridge, England: Cambridge University Press, 1971), 134.

23. Bruce Brown, *Marx, Freud, and the Critique of Everyday Life* (New York: Monthly Review Press, 1973), 12.

24. Georg Lukacs, *History and Class Consciousness*, trans. Rodney Livingstone (Cambridge, Mass.: MIT Press, 1971), 165.

25. Sennett and Cobb, *The Hidden Injuries of Class*, 23.

26. Ibid., 210.

27. Lerner, *Surplus Powerlessness*, 61.

28. Brian Jackson, *Working-Class Community* (New York: Frederick A. Praeger, 1968), 156.

29. Richard Balzer, *Clockwork: Life in and outside an American Factory* (New York: Doubleday & Co., 1976), 9.

30. Rubin, *Worlds of Pain*, 93.

31. Raines and Day-Lower, *Modern Work*, 56.

32. Ruth Sidel, *On Her Own: Growing Up in the Shadow of the American Dream* (New York: Viking Penguin, 1990).

33. Melvin Kohn, *Class and Conformity* (Chicago: University of Chicago Press, 1977), 66ff.

34. Sennett and Cobb, *The Hidden Injuries of Class*, 119ff.

3. Religion and the Realities of Class

1. Henry Mottu, "The Theological Critique of Religion and Popular Religion," *Radical Religion* 4:1 (1978), 5ff.

2. David Halle, *America's Working Man* (Chicago: University of Chicago Press, 1984), 268.

3. Tex Sample, *Blue-Collar Ministry* (Valley Forge, Pa.: Judson Press, 1984), 110.

4. Raymond Tiemeyer, "Words for the World: Classism and Language Malpractice," *LCA Partners*, February 1983: 22–23.

5. Max Weber, *The Sociology of Religion* (Boston: Beacon Press, 1963); first published in Germany in 1922.

6. Sample, *Blue-Collar Ministry*, 108, 127–31.

7. Martin Luther, *Small Catechism* (Philadelphia: Fortress Press, 1979), 4.

8. Paul G. Johnson, *Sunday/Monday Faith and Works Study* (Philadelphia: LCA Division for Parish Services, Department for Research and Studies, 1981).

9. Clifford Geertz, "Religion as a Cultural System," in *Religion and Ideology*, ed. Robert Bocock and Kenneth Thompson (Manchester, U.K.: Manchester University Press, 1985), 67.

10. Paul L. Wachtel, *The Poverty of Affluence* (New York: Free Press, 1983), 32, 44, 95.

11. "Americans Still Dream the American Dream," *Christian Science Monitor*, 2 March 1987: 21.

12. Pablo Richard, *The Idols of Death and the God of Life* (Maryknoll, N.Y.: Orbis Books, 1983), 12.

4. Theological Perspectives for Addressing Class Realities

1. John Francis Kavanaugh, *Following Christ in a Consumer Society* (Maryknoll, N.Y.: Orbis Books, 1981), 57.

2. Victorio Araya G., "The God of Strategic Covenant," in *The Idols of Death and the Gods of Life*, ed. Pablo Richard III.

3. Much of the above analysis is indebted to Rebecca Chopp, *The Praxis of Suffering* (Maryknoll, N.Y.: Orbis Books, 1986), 29–32.

4. Paul Tillich, *The Religious Situation*, trans. H. Richard Niebuhr (New York: Henry Holt & Co., 1932), 10.

5. Paul Tillich, *Political Expectation*, 1st ed., ed. James Luther Adams (New York: Harper & Row, 1971), 5–6.

6. Tillich, *Political Expectation*, 70.

7. Paul Tillich, *The Socialist Decision*, trans. Franklin Sherman (New York: Harper & Row, 1977), 101.

8. Chopp, *The Praxis of Suffering*, 1.

9. Ibid., 19.

10. Dorothee Soelle, *Political Theology*, trans. and intro. John Shelley (Philadelphia: Fortress Press, 1974), 61.

11. Lerner, *Surplus Powerlessness*, 230–31.

12. Matthew Lamb, *Solidarity with Victims: Toward a Theology of Social Transformation* (New York: Crossroad, 1982), 18.

13. Michael H. Taylor, "People at Work," in *Theology by the People*, ed. Samuel Amirtham and John S. Pobee (Geneva: World Council of Churches, 1986), 124.

14. Carl E. Braaten, "Praxis: Trojan Horse of Liberation Theology," *Dialog* 23 (Autumn 1984): 276–80.

5. The Domination of Sin

1. Martin Luther, *Luther's Works*, ed. Jaroslav Pelikan (St. Louis: Concordia Publishing House, 1956), 1:163, 159; 25:227; 26:310; 22:125.

2. John R. Loeschen, *Wrestling with Luther* (St. Louis: Concordia Publishing House, 1976), 55–56.

3. Scott H. Hendrix, *Luther and the Papacy* (Philadelphia: Fortress Press, 1981), xii.

4. Gregory Baum, *Religion and Alienation* (New York: Paulist Press, 1975), 201–2.

5. Ibid., 203.

6. José Miranda, *Marx and the Bible: A Critique of the Philosophy of Oppression,* trans. John Eagleson (Maryknoll, N.Y.: Orbis Books, 1974), 227.

7. Dorothee Soelle, *The Arms Race Kills Even without War,* trans. Gehard A. Elston (Philadelphia: Fortress Press, 1983), 87–92.

8. Dorothee Soelle, *Choosing Life,* trans. Margaret Kohl (Philadelphia: Fortress Press, 1981).

9. Beverly Wildung Harrison, "The Power of Anger in the Work of Love," in *Making the Connections,* ed. Carol S. Robb (Boston: Beacon Press, 1985), 14.

6. The Redemption
of American Working-Class Reality

1. Gustavo Gutiérrez, *A Theology of Liberation* (Maryknoll, N.Y.: Orbis Books, 1973), 167.

2. Jürgen Moltmann, *The Crucified God* (New York: Harper & Row, 1974), 195–96.

3. Juan Luis Segundo, *The Humanist Christology of Paul,* ed. and trans. John Drury (Maryknoll, N.Y.: Orbis Books, 1986), 132.

4. Gerhard O. Forde, "The Work of Christ," in *Christian Dogmatics,* ed. Carl E. Braaten and Robert W. Jenson (Philadelphia: Fortress Press, 1984), 2:50–51.

5. Segundo, *The Humanist Christology of Paul,* 131.

6. Dorothee Soelle, *Choosing Life,* 29.

7. Martin Luther, *Luther's Works,* 35:51–53.

8. Hendrikus Berkhof, *Christ and Powers,* trans. John H. Yoder (Scottsdale, Pa.: Herald Press, 1977), 21, 38.

9. See esp. Johannes B. Metz, *Faith in History and Society,* trans. David Smith (New York: Seabury/Crossroad, 1980).

10. Dorothee Soelle, *Suffering,* trans. Everett R. Kalin (Philadelphia: Fortress Press, 1975), 37.

11. Ibid., 76.

12. Mark Zima, unpublished journal (Lutheran School of Theology at Chicago, 1986).

13. Carter Heyward, *The Redemption of God: A Theology of Mutual Relation* (Washington, D.C.: University Press of America, 1982), 162.

14. Leonardo Boff, *Liberating Grace,* trans. John Drury (Maryknoll, N.Y.: Orbis Books, 1979), 37.

15. Martin Luther, *Luther's Works,* 27:266; although Luther predates our understanding of praxis, we contend that his theology is not antithetical to our intentions here.

7. Church as Midwife of New Communities of Justice

1. This notion is developed in books such as Sara M. Evans and Harry C. Boyte, *Free Spaces: The Sources of Democratic Change in America* (New York: Harper & Row, 1986).

2. Ibid., 201.

3. *Christianity and Crisis* 47:1 (2 February 1987) provides an excellent introduction to the principles and current examples of community organizing. See also Gregory F. Pierce, *Activism that Makes Sense* (Paramus, N.J.: Paulist/Newman Press, 1984).

Index

Index